TERENCE CONRAN
easy

living

conran
OCTOPUS

To help you have an easy and enjoyable life:

for Sebastian, Jasper, Tom, Sophie and Ned; Sam, Max, Finbar, Felix and Coco; Max, Toby and Harriet –
I hope you (and everyone else) will read the text as well as look at the pictures.

Commissioning Editor: Denny Hemming
Managing Editor: Richard Atkinson
Copy Editor: Helen Ridge

Design: Helen Lewis

Picture Research: Claire Taylor

Special Photography: James Mitchell
Special Photography Art Direction: Robin Rout

Production: Julian Deeming

Contributing Editor: Elizabeth Wilhide

Project Consultant: Simon Willis

Extracts from *How Proust Can Change Your Life*
by Alain de Botton are reproduced by permission of
Macmillan, London and Pantheon Books, New York.

Extracts from the works of Elizabeth David are reproduced
by permission of her Estate.

Extracts from *The Wind in the Willows* by Kenneth
Grahame © The University Chest, Oxford, reproduced by
permission of Curtis Brown, London.

First published in Great Britain in 1999
by Conran Octopus Limited
a part of Octopus Publishing Group
2–4 Heron Quays
London E14 4JP
www.conran-octopus.co.uk

This paperback edition published in 2002

© Conran Octopus Limited 1999

A catalogue record for this book is available from the
British Library.

ISBN: 1 84091 220 0

Colour origination by Sang Choy International, Singapore
Printed in China

contents

introduction 6

introduction

Whenever I am approached to give advice on interior design, I have a sneaking suspicion that what I am expected to provide is an instant set of style rules – a tried and tested formula that could be applied in every circumstance, guaranteeing 'perfect' results every time – or, at the very least, a list of my favourite colours and products for others to follow like a blueprint.

Instead, I usually answer that the first thing people should do is to take all of their possessions and pile them up outside their front door. Then, they should look long and hard at the basic shell that remains. Once this framework is right – when the spaces, the lighting, the services, the structure, the surfaces and finishes have been sorted out – then, and only then, should they think about which of their belongings to bring back indoors, keeping only those things that contribute something positive to their lives, whether aesthetically, emotionally or practically.

Of course, I am not seriously suggesting that every front garden up and down the country should suddenly be transformed into a reject pile ready for the skip, dump or boot sale – but I am only half joking. The basic attitude lying behind this superficially impractical strategy is one that I firmly believe to be important.

Where we live must work from the inside out, and from the ground up. This means taking where we are and who we are as starting points, not applying a set of arbitrary criteria dreamed up by somebody else. Only then can a home be a perfect fit, as comfortable as a favourite piece of clothing.

As modern life becomes ever more complex and fast paced, our homes must increasingly act as antidotes to stress and tension, as places to relax, unwind and be ourselves: essentially, as spaces for easy living. This function is not new: ever since industrialization,

the home has been a refuge, a necessary counterpoint to the world of work. What has changed, however, is that the need for space, privacy and comfort has become much more acute.

Easy living, however, is not about sinking into a mindless stupor. Living in a cocoon is one answer to the complexities and hardships of everyday life but it is ultimately a defensive, if not a negative stance. Instead, by 'easy' I mean the physical ease of simplicity, where practical tasks can be performed without frustration, fuss or muddle, where upkeep is straightforward and there is enough space and light to go round. This is largely, although not exclusively, a matter of getting the basic framework right. But, at the same time, 'easy' also implies the psychological freedom of coming through the front door and experiencing the sensation of kicking off your shoes – even if only mentally. This happens when your home provides room for self-expression and pleasure, when it feels like yours and not anyone else's and when it enables you to stay in touch with what you enjoy.

When it comes to easy living, rules only confuse the picture. Bombarded with advice and baffled by the myriad choices of the consumer world, establishing what you want and like is not so much a learning process, but more of a relearning process. It's a question of recognition. Focusing on those simple pleasures that make life worth living yet rarely stand out as high points in your personal history is enough to provide the direction you need. Sounds, smells and other less tangible triggers help to unlock the memory bank and identify what makes you feel good. Many of these elements will inevitably be common pleasures shared by us all, though no less important for that. Others will be more particular, related to a specific experience or event that has a personal meaning.

Easy living means opening your eyes to the beauty of everyday things, natural or man-made.

Vita Sackville-West, in a talk broadcast on BBC radio in 1950, identified a whole range of insignificant, essentially domestic pleasures that everyone has experienced from time to time but hardly ever remarks upon. In the family shorthand, which gave the talk its title, these brief moments of satisfaction were collectively termed 'through leaves', after the 'small but intense pleasure of walking through dry leaves and kicking them up as you go'. It was 'through leaves' to run a stick along an iron railing or to crunch thin ice; to suddenly remember a word or name you thought you'd forgotten; or to write with the perfect pen nib. So was pulling curtains that ran freely on their rods, sliding out the drawer of a steel filing cabinet which opened 'readily and silkily' on ball bearings, cutting pages of a book with a sharp paper-cutter, or drawing a cork with a good patent corkscrew. Drinking when you're thirsty, feeling sand between your toes at the seaside, reading in bed – that 'perfect moment' that lasts only as long as you can stay awake – sinking into bouncy seats at the cinema . . . . She concluded her talk by suggesting that her listeners come up with their own list of pleasures to add to those she had overlooked or forgotten.

It's an amusing exercise and a revealing one, as it shows how we don't necessarily have to go far and wide for our pleasures, since they are often right under our noses. Literally so, in many cases. A smell can be one of the most evocative spurs to the memory, conjuring rooms, events, periods of time we'd imagined that we had long forgotten. The wholesome smell of baking bread, the rich aroma of fresh coffee, the perfume of roses or lilies have an almost universal appeal, so much so that retailers often strategically employ such scents to whet the appetites of their customers. For me, it is damp earth in the rain or a fuggy greenhouse, cigar smoke, clean linen dried in the sun or the waft of pungent thyme on hot, dry Mediterranean air that summon up that same sense of well-being.

Enjoyable experiences are not always divisible into strict categories of sensation. Like Vita Sackville-West's 'through leaves', they come parcelled as snapshots of pleasure, where touch, sound, smell and sight all strike the same emotional chord – like waking up to find it has snowed overnight, shopping in an outdoor market, putting on a freshly ironed shirt or suddenly catching sight of the sea. I recently came across a café in Australia that filled me with an immense feeling of contentment, yet did so through very simple means. There was a big square table with people sitting casually round it drinking coffee and reading papers and, in the centre of the table, a large bowl of nobbly

Nothing tastes better or smells more appetizing than fresh food, simply prepared and quickly cooked outdoors. One of the pleasures of being on holiday is the opportunity to enjoy such basic meals, eaten as well as cooked in the open. It is easy enough, weather permitting, to enjoy the same directness of experience at home.

mons, with their leaves still attached. Nothing could be more straightforward or more suggestive of onviviality. It was a place where you simply wanted to sit down and join in. In the same way, the sight f a long table set up outdoors and covered with a white cloth can convey a mood of hospitality and elebration before the food is even laid out, while a crackling log fire — sight, smell, sound and warmth ll coming together in one focus — evokes an instant sense of security, comfort and nostalgia.

When you stop to consider, easy living is what most people want from a holiday. Once or twice a ear, we invest money in the quest for fine weather, good food, beautiful surroundings and an escape om all that makes life complicated and demanding. Two weeks later we are back at home, where the oliday spirit often wears off as fast as the suntan. There is no reason why this should be so.

The strong light of southern latitudes adds a particular vibrancy to colours. The many evocative blues of the Mediterranean and the hotter, spicier shades of Asia and Latin America appear more intense and more saturated there than under grey, northern skies. Or perhaps it is just a question of taking the time to look: when you are in the right frame of mind, colour sings out of details, no matter how insignificant they may at first seem.

Compartmentalizing life, so that contact with simple pleasures must be fitted into a scheduled slot, is the essence of modern alienation. The best souvenir we can bring back from holiday is the will to make everyday life more in tune with what we really enjoy.

Good holidays do not necessarily depend on exotic locations and luxurious accommodation, pleasurable though these may be. Many people choose to take their breaks in considerably simpler circumstances than those in which they live at home. Camping out in basic cottages or villas beside the sea or in the mountains, with only those belongings that fit in a suitcase or rucksack, coping with rudimentary facilities, stocking up at local markets and quaysides and passing days at a time without the intrusion of newspapers, television or a ringing telephone can be heaven on earth. Lying in the sun, swimming in the sea, taking brisk walks in the fresh air or even a good downpour replace the daily grind of commuting in stuffy trains, brooding at a computer terminal or sitting motionless in traffic jams. For people who choose to take such holidays, economy is far from being the most persuasive factor.

Easy living is about providing the means to experience thing directly, without the distancing intervention of technology or th burden of too many possessions. This is a salutary lesson in an ag when machines are assumed to be the panacea for many ills delivering convenience at the touch of a button, and when acquirin more and more material goods has become an aim in itself. Eas living on holiday, when we find that we can manage perfectly wel without nine-tenths of what our home contains, helps to remind u that machines break down, need servicing and maintenance an that possessions clamour to be organized, stored and looked afte When too much is on offer, we are beset by a series of nigglin choices that obscure real advantages of practicality and beauty.

Holidays also offer an essential breathing – and thinking - space. During a recent holiday, I read *How Proust Can Change You Life* by Alain de Botton. He describes how Proust encouraged discontented young man, frustrated by his dreams of palatial luxury to look at the still-life paintings of Chardin. By studying the everyda objects depicted – 'bowls of fruit, jugs, coffee pots, loaves of bread

On holiday, there is time to pay attention to more intangible elements, such as the quality of light. The grey, misty light of a northern seashore emphasizes the feeling of distance and the expansiveness of a sea view; while winter landscapes, with light reflected upwards from snow and ice, have a stark, graphic quality that accentuates form.

In steamy, tropical locations, outdoor living comes into its own. Owned by an American artist, this house in southern Sri Lanka (right), with its deep columned veranda and seating area among the palms, is perfectly in tune with its setting.

Rough painted plaster, terracotta and a bowl of fruit

offer the uplift of colour and textural character.

knives, glasses of wine, slabs of meat' – Proust believed the young man would realize he was already surrounded by beauty. In Chardin's paintings, such beauty was suggested in a 'harmony' between objects, for example, 'almost a friendship between the reddish colours of a hearthrug, a needle box and a skein of wool'. But it was also evident in the sensuality of visual experience that great painters can convey, such as 'the play of light on the end of the spoon, the fibrous softness of a tablecloth, the velvety skin of a peach'. Proust was demonstrating how happiness and contentment can come from learning a new way of looking at one's surroundings.

I cannot pretend, though, that easy living is necessarily doing it on the cheap. There is also a certain price to be paid in terms of work and time. Good materials that age well, thoughtful design and the finesse of detail tend to cost money and effort – but then, in the long run, so do shoddy products that break or wear out quickly and need to be replaced. And it can be just as expensive and laborious, if not more so, to repeatedly succumb to the marketable 'look' of the moment. The alternative – making choices by default, tinkering with problems rather than solving them, adopting second-best solutions because they are cheaper, haphazardly acquiring a collection of products and furnishings that say nothing and mean even less – often just results in a home that neither works very well nor feels right.

I have always felt that one of the greatest compliments a visitor to your home can pay you is to sit down and take off their jacket unprompted, to be as relaxed in your surroundings as you are. Yet how do you make it happen? To me, easy living in its widest sense is the natural by-product of good design. Although serendipity may come into it, it isn't completely accidental: on the contrary, comfort, simplicity, pleasure and practicality can come only from informed choice and creative application.

In the context of home design, choice has never been greater. But without a deeper understanding of why and how different elements work, choice can be meaningless. The design process itself can be seen as a series of choices, not, as is all too often supposed, choices based on looks alone, but a continual testing of parameters and weighing of alternatives. Beyond the superficialities of style are the essential qualities that make all the difference: the integrity of materials, the refinements of construction or manufacture, the inspiration of wit and imagination.

I believe that where and how we live is fundamental to our well-being; such considerations are too important to be sidelined into a holiday break and sidestepped the rest of the year. Things that work well, look beautiful, evoke memories and express our personalities restore quality to everyday living.

elements

The home is an emotional concept as much as a physical, serviced structure: bricks and mortar, plumbing and wiring, as well as comfort, security and well-being. Such states of mind, however, are not produced out of thin air. Providing the essential psychological context for enjoying everyday life is often a question of getting the physical framework in order. This means thinking about your home in a basic, elemental way. Space, light, colour, texture and material quality operate on many levels that go far beyond the practical.

We do not experience these elements in complete isolation. Space and light, light and air, colour and texture are intrinsically interwoven and connected. Nevertheless, each element has its own impact on the picture, which can be revealed dramatically in simple alterations that you make to your surroundings. Improving a lighting arrangement, for example, can transform a room from somewhere that makes you feel jaded or ill at ease for no readily identifiable reason into a place that is positively alive with vitality and warmth. Although the change may be accomplished on a physical level, with fittings, light sources and wiring, the effect is profoundly emotional.

Joseph Ettedgui, innovative retailer and fashion entrepreneur, believes that lighting and flooring are the two most important elements in the home and if these work, 'everything else will look wonderful'. Whenever he is creating a home, he always spends as much money as possible on good quality flooring, whether stone, wooden parquet or the softest carpet. 'The floor is one of the very first things you feel when you enter a place,' he says. 'Your feet actually feel quite a lot.'

Paying attention to basic elements can also mean making the effort to fix fundamental problems. Sometimes it is difficult enough to identify the problems in the first place. Here, time is both an ally and an enemy. We are all familiar with the odd feeling of walking through the front door after spending a few days away and seeing what are normally familiar surroundings in a new and not altogether uncritical light. In that brief window of opportunity, which may last only minutes, the defects that time has taught us to overlook are often suddenly glaringly obvious. But some shortfalls and deficiencies take a while to reveal themselves. You may have to live in a house for a considerable period of time to realize how best to improve it or undergo several changes of lifestyle before reorganization becomes a pressing concern.

Thinking about basic elements represents a kind of mental paring down. But it does not necessarily entail the rarefied contemplation of minimalism. For dedicated minimalists, space, light, colour and texture are not merely basic elements, they are the only elements. In buildings designed to provide such purity and perfection, the focus is entirely abstract. Things, however ordinary, are banished or hidden. And paradoxically, whenever objects are brought out to be used, no matter how unprepossessing they are, they can assume an almost distracting significance in the absence of anything else to look at. The result may indeed induce a Zen-like sense of peace and calm, as enthusiasts maintain, but at the considerable price of living in surroundings that constantly tell you what to do. I cannot help but feel that minimalism offers the enforced calm of the straitjacket, not the sense of ease I would naturally associate with being 'at home'.

In the public imagination, the term 'minimal' has become somewhat interchangeable with 'modern'. This is not altogether surprising, since there are clearly certain common denominators. While minimalism may be an uncomfortably extreme position for most people, it does reveal, like the best of modern architecture, the often unsung beauty of the

everyday – the play of natural light, the sheer dynamic of space and the subtleties of form and texture. Concentrating on these fundamentals is important, not least because they are so often overlooked. In the context of home design, many people tend to get obsessed by what is in the foreground, when the background may actually have a greater part to play. Realization often comes after the fact, when you can't think why you waited so long to make some simple alteration.

Minimalism offers another valuable insight, too, which is recognizing the irrelevance of a good deal of what fills our homes. Almost everyone could do with a little less in their lives. Here, a critical attitude is important to edit out what is surplus to requirements. This is not a case of making do with the bare minimum – unless you are that way inclined – but of weeding out what is redundant, ineffective or simply past the point where it is useful or meaningful.

There is a fine line that can be drawn between the clarity that modernism offers and the rather uptight nature of most minimal interiors. I've noticed that people who live in such formal surroundings have a tendency to rush off on holiday at the drop of a hat, searching, no doubt, for somewhere they can live a bit more easily. There's no denying that modern

can be easy, but not if it results in the kind of visual tenseness where furniture, fittings and interior space all share the same tight and angular aesthetic. If minimalism looks like it's hard work, that's because it often is. The best modern interiors, on the other hand, are liberating rather than constraining, freeing time and the imagination and putting the individual back firmly in the centre of the picture.

Most people, perhaps, can more readily imagine easy living taking place in an older house. It seems to go naturally with well-worn floors, generously proportioned rooms, sunlight flooding through sash windows and robust finishes that display the gentle mellowing of age. Older houses offer the comfort of familiarity and a sense of connection with both nature and history, a sense that is increasingly threatened in other areas of life.

The spatial issues that arise from living in a home with a past are of a different nature to those presented by the modern interior. In this situation, the question is frequently how to reconcile architectural character with the demands of contemporary living. Period houses can arouse extreme emotions in people – either the desire to rip out all historical

features and start anew, or the desire (much more common nowadays) to conserve or reproduce every minute detail down to the last fingerplate. Neither approach is particularly satisfactory. The former can be tantamount to vandalism; the latter forces you to live in an anachronism. Here, concentrating on the basic elements can help achieve a balance between an old framework and a modern lifestyle.

Buildings live longer than people and often outlast their original function, which makes an excessively preservationist attitude something of a nonsense. Subservience to the past can all too easily shade into pastiche and in the process what is truly timeless and appealing is lost. Loft living provides a good example of the benefits of creative transformation, bringing new life to perfectly serviceable structures – factories, schools, warehouses and so on – which would otherwise be redundant, and regenerating run-down areas of the inner city. In such cases, the answer is having the courage to combine old with new, marrying the depth of character that comes with the accretions of time with the sense of vitality that places you firmly in the here and now.

space

Without necessarily realizing it, we have an instinctive sense of proportion, derived from the natural world. In the 'Modulor' (above), a system of scale based on the dimensions of the human form, Le Corbusier attempted to provide a harmonious blueprint for design. The sweep of a stair and the vertical element of the column (left) have a natural echo in the towering uprights of the forest glade (right).

For most people, space means 'having enough room', as in space to put things or do things, or simply breathing space. The value of this increasingly precious commodity, however, cannot be measured merely in terms of quantity. What attracts us to certain spaces and not to others has more to do with abstract notions of proportion, balance and individual character than with the sheer elbow room of square feet and inches. The quality of space may be a concept that is difficult to articulate, but it plays a key role in our enjoyment of life.

Our attitudes to interior space are rooted in the natural world. It is not difficult to relate primitive shelters – tents, huts, tepees and igloos – to caves, groves of trees, caverns and other natural places of refuge. Not only are such vernacular structures typically built out of whatever materials are at hand; their scale and proportion often echo, whether consciously or not, natural harmonies.

The references to nature may be both literal and theoretical. The Greek temple, for example, has marble columns and lintels that have been carved to suggest earlier basic wooden forms of construction, while the orders of classical architecture are based on the 'golden section', where mathematical relationships can be found in the spiral form of galaxies, seashells, flowerheads and fir cones. The intuitive 'rightness' of such blueprints of design can be appreciated whether or not we have an understanding or even an awareness of the calculations. In the same way, the enduring appeal of symmetry can be traced to its familiarity as a pattern featuring prominently in nature.

It may seem an enormous leap from the hut to the high-rise apartment, but even modern architects, such as Le Corbusier, have attempted to base their designs on a natural system of scale. Le Corbusier's 'Modulor' took the human form as the basic index of dimension with the intention of bringing a universal harmony to design: 'proportion is the means to architectural lyricism' is how he termed it. We may not enter a room and subject it to that same intense level of analysis, but we know it when we feel it – when the basic proportion and disposition of space put us at our ease.

If spatial quality has much to do with a natural sense of proportion, it also provides a balance of emotional experience. Openness and enclosure, security and exhilaration, privacy and togetherness are all equally desirable and necessary.

At least part of the popularity of lofts and converted warehouses must be the fact that they offer the relatively rare opportunity to enjoy the almost giddy pleasure of life on a grand scale. When so much housing, old or new, has been designed to meagre spatial standards, finding yourself in a huge open expanse seems to promise infinite possibilities. Where such spaces are double-height, there is the added bonus of sweeping upward views, providing an uplifting sensation that normally one expects to experience only in public buildings and churches. It is this volume of space that generates the feeling of freedom, as much as the floor area.

Open space inspires a generous, inclusive approach to living. When barriers are down, activities can flow from one into another – from cooking to eating, from eating to relaxing – without the formal segregation implied by separate rooms. The planning of many of the houses we have inherited from the nineteenth century enshrine Victorian social distinctions between old and young, servants and masters, men and women, divisions that are no longer relevant or welcome. This strict spatial segregation also implies a hierarchy of activity, ranging from areas devoted to chores to areas set aside for near-indolence. Today, cooking may be work, but we expect it to be pleasurable work, part of the daily life of the whole household. Open space, whether it is achieved by converting an industrial building or knocking down walls in a Victorian terrace, allows everyone access to easy living.

Outdoor living areas restore a sense of connection with nature. With their elemental simplicity, the concrete table and benches sit easily in this garden (above).

Yet, as anyone who has tried to live in a single vast space will tell you, people also need places that are small and enclosed. In a warehouse conversion, this might simply be a partitioned area where you can shut the door and be by yourself. In other contexts, the enclosures may be smaller still: the alcove, box bed, window seat or chimney corner are traditional spatial patterns with an irresistible appeal. Self-contained, compact, secure and private, such features may not be practically necessary in the strictest sense, but they are hugely enjoyable.

For spaces to come alive, there must also be a sense of progression. This depends to a large extent on views and vistas that change as one moves from area to area or level to level. The staircase is potentially one of the most dynamic architectural features In this respect, but there are other means to the same end.

Balconies and generous openings such as French windows dissolve the boundary between indoors and out, half enclosed but open to light and air.

Designed by Andrew Patterson, this house (below), on a hill west of Auckland, New Zealand, has louvred panels that open fully to reveal the dramatic backdrop of a rugged landscape.

Courtyards, mezzanine levels, skylights, glazed internal doors or windows that allow glimpses from room to room, and other visual links between one part of a space and another or between indoors and out all generate an immense sense of vitality.

Assessing spatial quality can be difficult, particularly when one is so accustomed to the sort of standardized domestic planning common to most Western housing. This difficulty may account, in part, for the current fascination with feng shui, the ancient Chinese discipline that prescribes all manner of correct spatial alignments and placings to ensure good health, happiness and fortune. At present, feng shui is enjoying the full panoply of cult status and is the subject matter of countless books, magazines, newspaper articles and television programmes, and providing work for any number of consultants; nevertheless, that should not detract from the basic insights it has to offer.

While I am not temperamentally inclined to subscribe to the mystic rationale behind the practice of feng shui – the appeasement of good spirits or energies, the warding off of evil eyes – I can still appreciate the way in which these rules encapsulate many centuries' worth of observations on the sensitivity of human beings to their surroundings. I am not certain, for example, that I would be prepared to live with the constant tinkling of a wind chime, but I can recognize the fact that

for a wind chime to tinkle, there must be airflow, and the flow of air through a room, as opposed to the static, sealed atmosphere of a double-glazed office, is entirely beneficial and pleasurable. In feng shui, orientation is very important, with the Chinese preferring a north–south site, which, of course, is the best position for benefiting from solar power. In the same way, feng shui practitioners place great stress on furniture arrangement, recommending that desks be placed so they face an open door – which, as anyone can sense, is psychologically the most comfortable spot. A strategically positioned mirror (what one writer has called the 'aspirin of feng shui') may perhaps redirect the flow of ch'i, but it undoubtedly multiplies views and light. Flowers and other living plants may be remedies for every type of conceivable misfortune, from sharp protruding corners to over-scaled windows, but they also soften an interior by acting as living reminders of the natural world.

What constitutes bad feng shui is no less commonsensical. Homes that are poorly serviced, in need of repair or badly maintained have bad feng shui; clutter clogging up cupboards, attics and lurking under the stairs is also unpropitious. Feng shui encompasses many rules, from broad principles down to fine-tuning, but perhaps its most valuable contribution is the holism of the basic premise: that the quality of space and how we arrange it has a fundamental impact on our well-being.

The free flow of space in this house in Ahmadabad, India (above and right), designed by Le Corbusier, expresses perfectly his belief in the plan as the driving force in architectural design.

The 'enfilade' or symmetrical sequence through a suite of rooms is a classic spatial arrangement, dramatically enhanced in Trivancore Palace, India by a glossy black floor – a finish achieved, apparently, with egg white (above, far left).

Older houses were generally planned to segregate activities, with rooms assigned specific functions. Removing dividing walls allows living areas to flow more informally (above left).

Volume – as much as floor space – creates a thrilling feeling of expansiveness. In this loft-like conversion (left), internal windows provide commanding views across the living area.

A mezzanine level inserted within a large converted space maintains a sense of openness while offering a degree of privacy for sleeping (above).

In open-plan spaces, the positioning of furniture is of critical importance, setting up focal points of activity and creating circulation routes from one area to the next. This 'dining room' (above right) is defined solely by the placement of the table, chairs and fixed lighting.

Relaxed and informal, this sympathetic updating of an older house manages to retain an appealing architectural quality while making the most of views and natural light (right).

light

Light, more than any other element of the interior, generates mood and atmosphere: it has a direct line to the emotions. Sight is our most highly developed sense, and it is not surprising that light, which renders the world visible, should have such a profound effect on the way we feel. Given its central importance, however, it is curious that only a fraction of the effort and expense devoted to other aspects of decoration and furnishing is spent on lighting the home. One reason may be the fact that lighting is commonly perceived to be a difficult and technical subject that few of us could even attempt to understand; another may be that people have a tendency to get distracted by the various styles of light fittings available rather than consider the quality of light itself. Many homes are still both badly lit and overlit, which very often amounts to the same thing.

As is the case with space, thinking about light directs our attention back to the natural world. Human beings are instinctively drawn to the light, instantly revitalized by sunny days and oppressed by overcast skies. The annual summer migration of northerners to the warmer climates of the south can be seen as a quest for light; the popularity of package

holidays reveals this to be a very powerful craving. The identification of SAD (seasonal affective disorder) shows how serious the effects of light deprivation can be.

Bright sunshine is not the only enjoyable form of natural light, though. If you sit out of doors in the garden for any length of time, particularly in a sheltered spot, you will experience a series of minute variations of light levels and intensity. There may be crisply defined shadows when the sun is overhead, soft lengthening shadows towards the end of the day, patterns of dappled light and shade where the sun shines through the leaves of a tree, golden subfusc light as the setting sun catches on tiny dust particles in the air. It is these variations, as much as the mere fact that the sun is shining at all, that give pleasure.

More dramatic changes in the weather can also make you 'see things in a different light' – such as the sudden and ominous darkening that precedes a thunderstorm. In the same way, you can often sense that it has snowed overnight without getting up to look out of the window – the bright glare reflected up from the snowy ground generates a completely different quality of light. In southern California, the atmospheric

The simplicity of the paper lantern belies its effectiveness as one of the most evocative diffusers of light (above, far left).

Light becomes 'bluer' at twilight (above centre). **Artificial lighting should complement natural light levels, not act as a substitute.**

Dappled light, with its constantly moving patterns of light and shadow, generates a mood of immense well-being (above).

Natural light is always changing in colour, level, direction and intensity, from a dramatic stormy sky (right) **to the soft, rosy light of dawn. Artificial lighting should also achieve such variety.**

changes associated with smoggy conditions have given rise to the term 'airlight' to describe a diffused, generalized brightness. *L'heure bleue*, the French term for twilight, encapsulates perfectly that transitory time when the colour of light shifts towards the cool end of the spectrum. Artists from Turner to Hockney, who have a heightened sensitivity to such things, have often been attracted to a particular area of the world for the sole reason that it offers a different quality of light and thus a different way of perceiving colour.

Yet, no matter how aware people are of these differences, from moment to moment or latitude to latitude, that variety of light is all too rarely duplicated indoors. In place of the mobility of natural light, there is often a fixed, static central focus; in place of diffusion and subtlety, there is glare, and instead of intriguing patches of light and shade, there is uniform brightness which cancels out all depth of character. It is as if artificial light is only seen as a practical tool, a second-rate substitute for sunshine, with no aesthetic impact at all. Much more useful and ultimately more rewarding is to consider the quality of light in the interior overall, with natural and artificial sources working in partnership, which they do for much of the day and into the evening.

Living in northern latitudes, it is easy to assume that the more natural light a room receives the better – months of low winter sun and rainy weather make one greedy for as much sunlight as possible. It is no accident, for example, that Scandinavian styles of decorating seem designed to maximize the light, with pale airy colours, uncluttered windows and plenty of clear floor space. On the other hand, in areas of the world with more reliable weather, strong daylight, which can heat up an interior to an uncomfortable degree, is not as welcome. In warmer southern countries, there are wide verandas or shaded terraces to create temperate zones between indoors and out, smaller windows with deep embrasures to cut down the sun's penetrating glare, and screens, lattices and awnings to filter the brightness.

But attitudes to light are not necessarily determined simply by location; taste also has a part to play. It is striking that in eighteenth-century Europe, when developments in

Light reveals texture and form. Strong directional light casts crisp, defining shadows; gentle diffused side-lighting emphasizes the material quality of different surfaces.

As devotees of feng shui advocate, orientation can have a profound effect on the way you feel. Being awakened by sunlight is a gentler and more natural way of starting the day than by the shrill summons of an alarm clock.

technology and construction introduced the means to create large window openings fitted with relatively clear glass, houses were flooded with light and decorated in sympathy, while a mere century later, Victorian homes were characterized by a heavy gloom, with sombre colour schemes, heavy furnishings, windows shrouded in layers of fusty drapery and natural light treated almost as an intruder. Of course, gaslight, candles and oil lamps did dirty and darken rooms very quickly, and it was not until the advent of electricity that houses began to lighten up again; this clean source of power meant that for the first time paler decorating schemes could stay pristine for far longer periods of time.

For most of us today, light is the flip side of the spatial coin. We need space around us to appreciate the effects of light and we need light to reveal space. Travel to very different climates has also given us a taste for what bright light can do, and the result is a desire to make the most of whatever light is available at home. This can be achieved very simply by paying attention to orientation, so that activities benefiting from daylight take place in those areas of the home more likely to receive it. Enlarging or creating new windows and keeping window treatments unfussy will allow as much light as possible to be admitted; choosing the right colours and finishes will spread the light around and reflect it.

Such strategies for maximizing the effects of natural light are more or less obvious. It is natural light's partner – artificial lighting – that has a tendency to create more difficulties. When it was first made available to homes in the late nineteenth century, electrical lighting was perceived as extremely bright, although wattages were a fraction of what they are today. Since then, homes have been getting brighter and brighter, while at the same time, the number of light sources has decreased.

he end result is often an uncomfortable glare and a uniformity of effect that can
e extremely oppressive. Glare is the antithesis of easy living, and for very good
hysical reasons. It occurs when there is too great a contrast between a source of
ght and its surroundings, meaning that the eye has to make continual and
npleasant adjustments between the two. Uniformity – where all distinctions are
attened – is merely depressing.

   Artificial lighting does not have the same in-built variations that natural light
as and which makes it so appealing. No matter how much natural light a room
eceives, the effect will never be static, simply because the colour, direction and
ntensity of light are changing constantly as the sun makes it way across the sky.
Vhen you are creating an artificial lighting scheme, you have to work that much
arder to provide an equivalent richness of experience.

**In northern latitudes, where
there can be many months of
grey skies, we need as much
natural light in the interior as
possible. High-level arched
windows flood the space with
pure light in this house designed
by the minimalist architect
Claudio Silvestrin** (above)**.**

Much can be done simply by increasing the number of light sources in a room, at the same time decreasing the intensity of each light. One bright ceiling light may well supply all the light you need to see by, but it will not provide the right quality of light to live by. A variety of dimmer light sources at different heights and angled in different directions, on the other hand, is immediately comfortable and atmospheric. Each light on its own is not bright enough to hurt the eyes, but the sum total of illumination is still the same. And in place of a flat, even level of light, there are overlapping pools of brightness and shade that enhance form and texture. It may be light that we are drawn to, but it is shadow that makes things interesting.

Direction of light is another key factor. Light upwards – so that light bounces off the ceiling – and you create a sense of expansion. Light sideways, and you graze surfaces, revealing contour and texture. Light downwards

and you pick out a page, a keyboard, a worktop or an object in a tight focus of attention. Combine some or all of these in one particular area and you begin to create a sense of vitality.

The enormous range of light sources that are now on the market also enables you to experiment with colour. Tungsten, which is certainly still the most common of all domestic light sources, gives off a warm, golden cast that is inherently domestic. It is also more than a little familiar, as it comes most closely to matching the colour of candlelight.

In recent years, halogen lighting has become far more widely available for use in the home. Crisp and white

Warm light is reassuring, intimate and hospitable. Firelight is as warm psychologically as it is physically, while the golden light of dusk completely saturates colours. Tungsten light, which has a rich golden cast similar to candlelight, is both welcoming and flattering.

and with the ability to render colours nearly as faithfully as daylight, halogen introduces yet another dimension to the lighting repertoire. Adding a dimmer system to such lights also gives you the option of changing the mood and quality of light still further as early evening shades into dark night.

In the context of lighting, what works aesthetically is not far removed from what works on a practical basis. Good functional light is glare-free and often directional. It illuminates the task at hand without shining in your eyes or causing distracting reflections on the periphery. It is bright enough, but not over-bright. And like all forms of servicing, it is only as good as its infrastructure. Flexibility is that much easier to achieve when there are enough power points and well-positioned controls.

Quality of light is critical for easy living. Whether it is the midday sun slanting through half-closed venetian blinds, the warm, intimate circle of light spilling from a shaded table lamp, the boost to concentration from an angled work lamp, the hospitality of dancing firelight and flickering candlelight, or the dappled light of a shaded veranda or terrace, light is one of the most engaging of basic elements.

Rooms with more than one aspect, where natural light comes from different directions, have an innate sense of vitality (below). The effect is especially pronounced if windows are on adjacent, rather than opposite, walls. As the sun changes position in the sky, the level and direction of light shift accordingly.

Colour is a key consideration when planning a lighting scheme. Halogen light sources have a cool, white tone, similar to daylight, while tungsten, the standard domestic light source, and candlelight are much warmer and more intimate.

Colour is detail in this minimalist interior. Incidental objects – such as flowers, paintings, even people – can all provide vivid accents when the backgrounds are pure or neutral.

Vivid cushions provide a visual treat and a human touch in a restrained modern interior (right).

All dyes originally came from natural sources, whether animal, vegetable or mineral (above). Natural dyes can result in tones as soft as the earthy flecks of tweed or as searing as the vibrant hues of India. Textiles that have been dyed or coloured naturally fade gracefully with time and repeated washing.

The inspiration for colour is everywhere: the landscape, flowers and even food can all be the starting point when choosing colours to live with.

Colour depends on context, in particular the conditions of natural light. Coloured glass is particularly evocative as it dapples surfaces with intensely coloured shadows.

Nature provides many surprising colour combinations; the patterns on the wings of butterflies were my childhood passion.

Red is the luckiest colour for the Chinese, symbolizing happiness and strength, while yellow means long life. Feng shui practitioners regard all-white rooms as invitations to disaster; what we might find chic and sophisticated, they believe encourages serious illness. We ascribe our own positive and negative emotions to colours: red is for anger, debt and seduction; green for envy and 'go'; yellow for cowardice and constancy; blue for purity, freshness and depression. Designers of packaging and logos pay extremely close attention to such meanings, and manufacturers and retailers profit by them.

On the purely physical side, we have in-built sensitivities to certain colours which derive from wavelength patterns. In daylight conditions, our eyes naturally find colours in the middle of the spectrum – from yellow to green – easiest to see. Green, therefore, is literally relaxing and restful, whether it is the green of a garden or landscape or the pale green on the walls of an operating theatre where it provides the least distracting environment for life-or-death surgery.

As daylight begins to fade, the range in which we see most easily shifts slightly to blue. Red, on the other hand, is anything but restful. While blue is the colour of coolness and distance, red is warm and advancing. It is both nature's alarm bell and lure, signalling the poisonous berry and the ripe apple; it stimulates action. It will grab a baby's attention as quickly as a shopper's.

How the perception of colour is affected by light and, in turn, how colour affects our perception of space, is critical when it comes to decorating and furnishing the home. Pale colours, which have a lot of white in them, reflect light and spread it around; dark colours, on the other hand, are more enclosing and light-absorbent. But a great deal depends on context. Blue, for example, can be airy and inspirational, its distancing effect increasing the sense of spaciousness. However, in a room that receives little direct sunlight, the same shade can appear cold, clinical and downright depressing. Red can be warm, welcoming and cheerful, but in large doses it is simply exhausting, too much of a good thing.

Certain shades that hover on the brink between one colour and the next, such as blue-green, grey-blue, orangey-red and reddish-blue, change dramatically at different times of the day – luminous variations that can be a useful way of

Blue is the colour of distance and expansion – think of the sea and the sky. In the interior, it has the effect of increasing the sense of spaciousness, but it needs to be used in areas where the quality of natural light is good, otherwise the effect can be clinical and enervating. Here, blue defines a kitchen wall in a space well lit by a glazed roof (centre). By contrast, red is an advancing colour that attracts the attention and adds vitality. What might be tiring on a grand scale makes an unbeatable accent.

introducing a sense of vitality to your surroundings. Picking out a component of one of these hybrid shades to use as an accent, for example setting blue against reddish-blue, often has an invigorating edginess, while pale grey-blue backgrounds seem to make other colours sing out. What are properly termed complementary colours, that is those that sit opposite each other on the colour wheel, such as red and green or blue and orange, tend to make stimulating partnerships. Studying colour theory is one route to such discoveries; even better is taking the trouble to look – at nature, in particular. My boyhood passion for moths and butterflies introduced me to unimaginable combinations of colour and pattern as did my ambition to collect and press every wild flower in the land. I couldn't have had a better introduction to the impact of colour contrast than that offered by one of my earliest colour memories – seeing bright green paint spilled on a terracotta-tiled floor.

It is important to remember that rooms can be colourful even when the walls are painted white – perhaps the commitment implied by painting all four walls the same shade is part of what scares people off in the first place. Joseph, the fashion entrepreneur, loves colour, but believes that mixing different colours successfully is actually a very difficult skill to master. Rather than make a mistake, he keeps the backgrounds in his home soft and muted, neutral tones against which the vibrant shades of flowers, fruit and clothing can stand out. The spines of books, a painted door, plastic beakers, intriguing packaging, coloured glass vases, cushions and throws, flowers, paintings, even people in the room can contribute substantial jolts of colour, visual treats that the eye returns to again and again – and that's my philosophy on colour, too. Colour, in this sense, can just happen, and the result is often far more refreshing and joyous than the most carefully planned and coordinated scheme.

Texture alters our perception of colour. Rugged, matt or grainy surfaces tone down the intensity of different shades, while glossy, polished or reflective surfaces add definition and vibrancy. Natural materials, such as wood, terracotta and rough plaster, come in an inherently gentle palette of earthy, companionable tones, all of which work well together.

texture

Texture connects us with the physical world where materials have weight and resistance, surface and finish. In the pattern of grain or drape of a cloth, texture acts as a reminder of how things are made, by man and by nature.

In the context of interior design, the visual importance of texture is widely stressed. Texture, as a variable of colour, can soften or sharpen a tone – you only have to consider the contrasting impact of matt, satin and gloss paint finishes.

As an intrinsic element of pattern, texture emphasizes movement and rhythm, evident in the direction of a weave or the twist of a pile. In fact, it is arguable that patterns that have some foundation in texture, such as damask and brocade, have more inherent vitality than those that are simply surface printed. Variations between smooth and rough and ridged and plain introduce a sense of definition and character, revealed as light is reflected off the surface of the fabric, or shadows fall into hollows and indentations. The simpler the surroundings, and the more subdued the colours, the greater the role that texture has to play.

But what texture can do for the appearance of a room is only a part of the story. Seeing is not always believing, which explains why we like to squeeze fruit on a market stall, finger the nap of a suit hanging on a shop-rail or stroke the surface of a sofa. Texture always implies and invites touch, from the tips of the fingers to the soles of the feet; the tactility of the materials we live with contributes profoundly to the pleasure we derive from using them. A polished wooden banister, an earthenware pot, painted brickwork, a nubbly rug, a scrubbed oak table and a porcelain cup may all share the same neutral tones, but they offer widely different experiences the minute they are encountered directly.

Variations of texture add character and tactility to this interior (right). **The smooth spindles of the chair backs invite touch, as do the terracotta urn and woven objects, placed where the light reveals the quality of their surfaces.**

Wood grain, evident in unfinished beams and columns or in smooth veneer, has a direction and pattern that serve as a reminder of the living origin of the material.

Hard, reflective metal panels, appliances and door fronts sharpen the look of working areas like kitchens. Metal brings a chic contemporary edge to the home, borrowed from industrial contexts such as factories and laboratories – though nature, too, offers a similar palette of colours.

Natural materials age well, acquiring a pleasing character over years of handling and use.

Texture draws in other senses, too. The hollow echo of floorboards when you walk on them, the chink of glass, the rustle of silk are the aural evidence of material quality. Here, as in other areas, sensations overlap: the clubby smell of leather is indivisible from the warm grainy feel of hide; the sharp tang of new wood is as instantly identifiable as whorls and knotholes.

On this sensual, emotional level, contrast is also critical. An environment that was seamless and smooth would be curiously dislocating and other-worldly, while one that was entirely rough and unyielding we would naturally read as a fairly hostile place – you only have to compare the experience of walking in a natural landscape with walking in a shopping mall or along an asphalted road. Real terrain offers a rich variety of experience underfoot, from dry, shifting leaves to bouncy turf, from the slow drag of sand to the tense grip of rock. Uniform urban environments, such as relentlessly smooth terrazzo or concrete, tire the mind as much as the feet.

Of equal importance is that textural variety can satisfy our innate desire for change and stimulation without setting thoughts flying in every direction. An excess of visual distraction, where everything is clamouring for attention – too

many colours, too much clutter, too much decorative detail – can all too quick[ly] send you into overload. Variety of surface and finish, however, is far more insinuati[ng] and subtle; it registers on a less conscious plane.

If texture is a way of grounding everyday experience, it also provides a w[ay] of authenticating materials. I am not a huge fan of synthetic products, even thou[gh] I can appreciate the vibrant, luminous colours and organic forms that can [be] achieved in plastics, and relish their use for their own sake. In general, howev[er] mass market synthetics always seem to be a bit of a cheat, promising a look-ali[ke] quality without the more tangible dimensions of the real thing. The deception is [for] your eyes only. You only have to walk on a vinyl floor or touch marbleized tiles sleep in polyester sheets or eat off a laminate table to notice the difference. Th[e] floor will sound tinny, the tiles will be warm to the touch, the sheets will not breat[he] and the tabletop will be scratchy.

What I dislike most about artificial materials is their inability to age in a[n] agreeable way. Real, natural materials, derived from plants, animals or the ear[th] seem to retain the same ability to change that one associates with living thing[s]

Textural quality contributes profoundly to the pleasure we derive from everyday activities. The smoothness of glass and porcelain makes tumblers and cups a delight to hold and sip from, just as a polished banister invites you to run your hand along it. The subtle textural contrasts of wood, stainless steel and stone flooring offer a variety of tactile, acoustic and visual experiences – differences that register on an almost subconscious level but which are no less important for being unemphatic.

e ageing process, provided there is a degree of care and maintenance, is always the better. Connoisseurs of antique furniture wax lyrical about patina, the depth d character that comes of years of sympathetic handling, care and use; it is rather ficult to imagine synthetic products, which either stubbornly refuse to grow old, do so in the most unappealing way, attracting such a degree of affection in cades to come, although I have to admit that sixty-year-old Bakelite does appear have achieved cult status.

Texture is the most obvious way such distinctions are conveyed. A flagged or, worn by the relentless tread of feet, linen sheets repeatedly washed to a silky ftness, solid tabletops scrubbed and polished, smooth beachstones battered by e tide – all enshrine the passage of time, a continuity that is deeply reassuring d comfortable. I would never decry the new, or surround myself, as some people , only with objects that have a respectably long pedigree. But materials that have s in-built capacity to wear well and grow old gracefully seem to me to be the sence of easy living, simply because they are so inherently tolerant. Fading from e sun, and all the other gentle discolorations and marks of time tend to inspire

affection rather than revulsion. When the material has a natural source, it's easy to put up with such minor imperfections, even grow to like them, and where everything shares the same capacity to mellow, the overall effect is bound to be sympathetic. By contrast, materials that trick you at the essential point of contact and unnervingly shrug off all signs of use or require constant vigilance to maintain their pristine condition add work, stress and a sense of unreality to your life. Although they are often promoted as labour-saving, the very reverse is often the case. It is also important to consider that synthetic materials are at their best on day one and can go downhill fairly rapidly thereafter.

Textural quality, and indeed variety, require a certain investment of time and money. Natural materials are usually more expensive than their synthetic counterparts, whose economy is often their most persuasive selling point. Real, natural materials can also be demanding in terms of care and maintenance, although it must be said that the effort expended in this regard is always repaid by a pleasing renewal of character and finish. Such choices are to be made for the economic long run and for your long-term contentment.

This house in Ahmadabad, India (left), designed by Le Corbusier, reveals a masterful play of surface and finish, with exposed brick walls contrasting with the dramatic grid of local stone flooring. Textural quality is often associated with vernacular buildings, where materials are natural in origin and sourced locally, such as whitewashed stone and brickwork, timber panelling and cladding; these materials can also be used to add character to more contemporary settings.

comfort

Comfort is one of those concepts that comes more sharply into focus when looked at the other way round — we all know what discomfort is. A couple of stops down from the acute emergency of pain, discomfort is water seeping into your shoes, crumbs in the bed, a nagging ache somewhere unimportant, a nasty draught, a noxious smell, a filthy taste, a sticky social situation . . . . Rooted in the physical, but not exclusively of the body, discomfort signals any kind of imperfect fit between ourselves and our surroundings.

Absence of comfort is not life-threatening. Indeed, whole centuries have passed without people giving it much thought, being for the most part rather more preoccupied with the stark realities of getting enough to eat or, at the top of the social scale, with simply showing off. Comfort did not begin to be designed into our lives until there was enough leisure to enjoy it. The court of Louis XV saw the introduction of the first upholstered furniture, padded, curved and angled to accommodate the human frame in repose, while at a similar time in England the notion of comfort became identified with a whole culture of domestic contentment. Comfort has had these two sides, tangible and intangible, ever since.

Perhaps it is something to do with the Protestant work ethic, or simply the lingering traces of a puritanical sensibility, but many people still regard comfort as something of an indulgence, the soft option that tempts you from the straight and narrow. I would argue that truly comfortable surroundings, where the lighting is set at just the right level, possessions are within easy reach, furniture supports your body and everything functions as it should, provide the best environment for creativity. This is not a view, I know, that is shared by many artists and writers who firmly uphold the belief that the garret life is essential for inspiration.

Comfort is a notoriously elastic term and inherently subjective, which may be part of the problem. If you consider basic physical parameters, for example something as seemingly specific as a comfortable temperature, it's hard to get two people to agree, even when they live under the same roof. One will always be turning up the heating or pulling on a jumper, while the other is opening an window and complaining how hot it is. It is the same with broader notions of comfort. Everyday life is unquestionably more comfortable today than it was in the distant past; indeed, we now take quite a high degree of comfort for granted. Few people in the West expect to have to break the ice in a washbasin first thing on a winter's morning, for example, or to sleep on a lumpy straw mattress. Comfort in this sense is also comparative, a way stage on the route between necessity and luxury.

Can you have too much of a good thing? Where comfort is taken as read, discomfort can suddenly seem more meaningful, even worthier, a sort of grit in the oyster theory. Perhaps I just don't like to feel uncomfortable if I can avoid it, but it seems to me that there is only a short step from believing that comfort somehow gets in the way of thinking about higher things and putting on a hair-shirt. Certainly, the degree of indulgence that swaddles, cocoons or insulates the senses can so easily lull you into a near-vegetative state; pulling back from such overprotection may be the only way to remind yourself that you are still alive. But, again, it comes back to the way you define it. I see comfort less in terms of an extra cushion or slightly softer pillow and more as a state of equilibrium, a balance that is ultimately as liberating for work and self-expression as it is naturally pleasurable. For Joseph, too, comfort is a balance: 'Everything has got to be very relaxed but at the same time not so loose that one doesn't care.'

In the popular imagination, comfort is often confused with luxury. As architectural critic Jonathan Glancey pointed out in a recent article, 'luxury' is an appendage that is increasingly tagged on to a huge range of incredibly ordinary items in an attempt to persuade people to buy things they don't need or to persuade people that the things they do buy are exceptionally distinguished. I very much prefer his definition of luxury: '. . . a walk along a deserted beach . . . a house with stone floors in the heat of an Italian summer . . . having a day to yourself reading a book . . . lying in bed on a working day, rain beating against the window, a pot of tea and a pile of magazines and newspapers . . . .' And, of course, a cigar.

What makes the chef John Torode feel most comfortable is being able to sit down and read a book with his children, or working hard in the garden; it is definitely not the boring regimentation of the comfort zone 'where you are lounging in a chair reading the papers between the hours of nine and ten on a Sunday morning'. For Suzie Slesin, the design editor of the American magazine *House & Garden*, it is having 'no hands-off places' so that you don't have to worry constantly about something breaking or getting dirty.

Our daily lives are full of stress, much of which is unavoidable. I believe that if our homes cannot provide some kind of refuge or respite from that stress, both physically and emotionally, then they have failed in one of their most critical functions. From supporting the body at rest or during relaxation — physical comfort at its most basic — to elemental pleasures that put people at their ease, comfort provides a necessary sense of renewal. For me, comfort is neither mindless luxury nor suffocating indulgence: it is the essential breathing space in which we can simply be ourselves, surrounded by the things we really like rather than the things we think give us status.

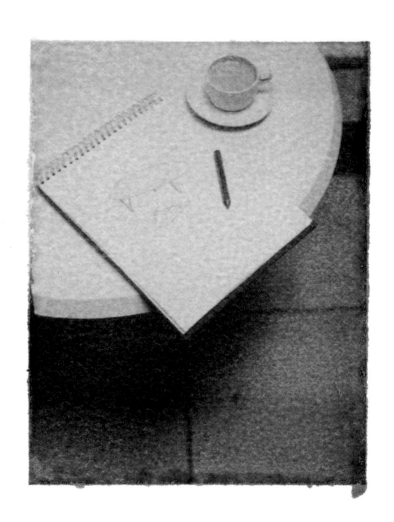

relax

Providing a place to relax is one of the most importan[t] functions a home can fulfil today. The speed of communication[s,] the frustrating slowness of traffic, the incessant intrusion o[f] stimuli from television, phones, newspapers and compute[r] networks mean that many people find themselves on constan[t] alert. Days filled with appointments that shade into evening[s,] answering phone messages and juggling commitments hav[e] little slack in them. But you cannot live in a state of battle[] readiness for ever. When it all gets too much, and preferabl[y] well before breaking point, you need to recharge you[r] batteries, take stock – or, in the French phrase, *reculer pou[r] mieux sauter*: 'pull back to leap further'.

It takes time to unwind and when time is limited, yo[u] need all the help you can get to find the mental and physica[l] room to let go. Spaces designed, arranged and furnished fo[r] easy living won't necessarily unclutter your diary, but the[y] may keep you sane. The shift of gears into more comfortabl[e] surroundings acts as a kind of daily 'downshifting', a reminde[r] that there are other ways of looking at things.

In theory, you should be able to relax almost anywher[e] in the home, but curiously the room that should provide th[e] right environment for relaxation often conspicuously fails i[n] this department. If you do most of your living away from th[e] living room, something is going wrong somewhere.

Ghosts of former roles haunt many living rooms today[.] In the rigid hierarchy of Victorian society, the parlour was [a] public receiving room, decorated and furnished to impress[.] Well into this century, it was not uncommon for the sittin[g] room or 'front room' to be kept more or less sealed until th[e] next visitor arrived – in some households, it took a birth[,] wedding or funeral for the room to be opened to view[.] As a showcase, the sitting room was a place for prize[d] possessions, wedding presents and the best furnishings [a] family could afford, but the trouble was that hardly anyon[e] ever got to see them, much less use them. They were ther[e] primarily as a marker of status.

Living rooms are rarely kept under wraps these days –[] who could afford to lose so much space? – but something o[f] this formal, hands-off status-seeking quality often lingers[.]

Comfort implies mental and physical breathing space – and that means surroundings where you can unwind, be yourself and spend at least some time doing very little of consequence. In a café near the Champs-Elysées, I once watched an elderly lady order a pear for dessert and then proceed to pare it slowly and expertly with a knife until the skin uncurled in a single spiral – a delicate performance of dexterity and concentration that must have been as relaxing to execute as it was to observe.

It is impossible to relax in room where furnishings require constant vigilance to remain in pristine condition or where everything says 'don't touch'. In this simple Australian house (left), once the home of my daughter Sophie and her husband Alex Willcock, flagston flooring, rammed earth walls and a raftered ceiling make a basic background, domesticated by a vivid chequered quilt hanging on the wall, natural fibre matting and white loose covers. My own home in the south of France (right) is also a converted farmhouse, where the simplicity of the stone flooring and plain whitewashed walls has been tempered by a layer of comfort in the form of cushions, throws and a rug.

Although we may live in a much looser and more democratic culture today, it seems we haven't quite tamed our desire to show off. I think that rooms furnished with an eye to what the neighbours will think often end up being places no one enjoys very much. Keeping up appearances generates a kind of starchy atmosphere, which is far from comfortable; yet, ironically, the very last thing most people want, either for themselves or their guests, is to feel uneasy.

Rooms that are sending out all the wrong messages are one thing, but in many living areas the messages are far from clear. We know what kitchens and bathrooms are used for and the bedroom's role is self-evident. But, in many homes, living rooms simply accommodate what is left over, mopping up a series of activities and objects that may be entirely unrelated and fundamentally incompatible. Far from being

a place to relax, the living room turns into a zone that requires constant mediation. Here, there are two approaches you can take. You can be ruthless, decide what you really want the space to provide and replan your home so that all those objects that don't fit into the scheme of things go elsewhere or are disposed of. Alternatively, you can open the space up further, so that a natural flow of activity can take place. After all, it can be just as relaxing to cook a meal as to listen to music, and in an open-plan area there is no reason why you can't do both. Such spaces are inherently welcoming, because they offer the hospitable sense of being drawn into the life of the household.

How then do you set about creating relaxing and welcoming surroundings? The first step is being able to recognize exactly what it is that makes you feel at ease.

If I were to imagine the type of room that would make me fe comfortable and completely relaxed, it would contain a bi squashy sofa upholstered in creamy white, roomy wick chairs with large, crumpled cushions and a well-worn stor floor covered with a beautiful rug. White linen curtains wou flutter gently at open windows, admitting shafts of sunlig and wonderful views – the sea or a river in one direction ar a lush green landscape in the other. There would be a fire the fireplace, logs barely alight, so that the smell woodsmoke drifted through the room. A carafe of win generous tumblers and a big bowl of French breakfa radishes would be set out on a scrubbed wooden table, an a large Morris Louis would be hung on the wall. I would b dressed in faded worn clothes (no tie) and a pair of m favourite leather slippers (no socks).

Those are the sort of surroundings that would please ⋯e. It stands to reason that if you please yourself, you are far ⋯ore likely to make others feel welcome and comfortable, ⋯o, and the result will be the opposite of a room that puts ⋯eryone on their best behaviour. Comfortable seating, the ⋯ght level of lighting and enough space to move around freely ⋯e obviously parts of the equation. And, since informality ⋯es hand in hand with outdoor living, some connection with ⋯arden areas will bring in a spirit of freshness and vitality. On ⋯arm days, you want to be able to open windows and doors ⋯d venture out as the mood strikes. Furnishings that are ⋯qually at home indoors or out are not only inherently simple, ⋯ey underscore this sense of connection.

In the city, we spend much of the time in a state of ⋯efensiveness, closing our ears to the blare of traffic, trying

not to breathe in polluting fumes and turning our eyes away from the harsher sights of the urban environment. Relaxing means learning to let the barriers come down. Outdoor living provides the surest shortcut to re-engaging with the physical world and finding pleasure in it again; nature is unsurpassed in its ability to calm us down. A hammock slung between the branches of a tree, a simple table set up under vine-covered trellis, a garden seat surrounded by scented planting, a few fat cushions and a blanket thrown down in a grassy spot offer a directness of experience that is a real clue to easy living and well worth emulating inside the home.

The sounds, smells and sights we enjoy in nature provide valuable clues for creating the relaxing and comfortable spaces in which to live. One of the most soothing sounds that I know is the trickle of water in a garden pool.

Creative daydreaming can help identify the situations and places that make you feel the most relaxed. The sound of running water or waves breaking on the shore is incredibly relaxing, which may help to explain why fishing is such a popular sport. Although it would be impossible, not to mention undesirable, to divert a trout stream through your living room, it is important to pay attention to the quality of sound and to make the most of opportunities to connect indoors with out.

Relaxing outdoors can be as basic as lying on a blanket under a shady tree or rocking gently in a hammock, while some of the most pleasant places of all are those indoor/outdoor areas, such as verandas and terraces, that are half-sheltered and half-exposed. Inside, there is no reason why rooms for relaxing should not display the same spontaneity and informality.

While few of us would want to install a fountain in the living room, it is important to pay attention to the quality of sound. Uniformly hard surfaces will result in a clattering environment full of grating noise, where the smallest movement is amplified to an uncomfortable degree, while heavily carpeted spaces, layered in fabric, have the muffled, deadened feel of a padded cell – the absence of sound can be strangely unnerving. A balance between resonant surfaces and finishes and sound-insulating ones, plus plenty of airflow to stir and rustle create an aural environment that is stimulating without being overwhelming.

Smell, our most evocative sense, is no less influential in shaping our mood. A scent is fleeting; it is estimated that we specifically notice all but the most pungent and noxious odours for mere seconds following our first exposure to them, after which time, we simply get used to them. This accounts for the critical importance of the threshold as a zone for enticing consumers into a shop, restaurant or supermarket; in some enterprises, appetizing smells of freshly baked bread and roast coffee are now synthesized and piped to strategic points to encourage spending – even new luxury cars are now sprayed with the smell of leather. At a time when fresh food is commonly sold sealed in layers of plastic, grown for appearance not flavour or aroma, and baking takes place in a distant factory, this seems exceptionally depressing and cynical to me. A good smell should be evidence of authenticity and quality; when we set out to analyse the particular smell of The Conran Shop, we found it to come from products, such as coffee, soap and wooden tables rubbed with linseed oil, that we were actually selling. In the home, too, the smells that greet you and continue to exert their subtle influence on a less immediate level should testify to the natural qualities of materials and finishes. Real materials often benefit from being maintained in an equally natural way, with traditional oils, waxes and cleansers rather than synthetic wonder products that promise instant

sults and leave the penetrating odour of ersatz pine, lemon or rose lingering in the air. Herbs planted a sunny spot near the back door, freshly cut flowers, tomatoes ripening on a sill, something good to eat the oven – these are hospitable, homely smells that do not come in a spray can.

If you focus on such basic elements, and take the lead from them, you are more likely to arrive at urroundings that express your personality and pleasures. What will be on view will reflect your tastes, ur 'style' and not one you have imported from a television programme or the pages of a magazine.

Inevitably, on prominent view in many living areas there are computers, televisions and sound systems. uch technological intrusions can be strikingly at odds with the way the rest of a room looks: large black oxes and their accessories will quickly dominate the most sympathetic interior. Most of us, no matter ow high-minded we pretend to be, are not going to forgo some form of in-house entertainment, but it is ell worth looking for compact designs that blend in less obtrusively; with the miniaturization of technology, small size represents no compromise in performance these days. While the television screen does need be big enough for comfortable viewing, there are designs that are attractive enough not to be hidden way in cupboards: Philippe Starck's 'Jim Nature' television, in its recyclable casing, for example, introduces n element of tactility to this familiar piece of technology. Place the television so that it is in a good viewing osition for the times you switch it on, but so that it is not occupying pride of place as a focal point. Perhaps you have done your job properly and created a space that is truly relaxing, you will find yourself less clined to switch on the box in the first place.

It goes without saying that however you choose to relax, it can only take place when the body is omfortable. Sitting or lounging on the floor can be very restful, but most of us in the West cannot maintain uch postures for any length of time. This means that furniture design has a critical role to play.

Comfort may be hard to define, but most of us know it when we feel it, hence the popularity of bouncing n beds and sinking into sofas in furniture showrooms. Designers, however, have to start somewhere, and hysical parameters begin to give shape to the idea. It is small wonder that chairs and sofas have arms, acks and legs just like we do. In a comfortable sofa, the angle or rake of the back answers the curvature f the spine, padding shields our bones from the rigid framework beneath, arms support our arms. We either slump nor sit too upright. In an uncomfortable sofa, the hollow in the small of the back meets a acancy, or the body slides forward to rest on the tailbone. Arms are high and dry, backs ache, breathing constricted and we sink inevitably into a stupor.

The design process begins prosaically, with reference to anthropometric guidelines setting out basic uman dimensions. Full-size sectional drawings are worked up on paper or screen; scale models add the hird dimension, but for an assessment of comfort, there's no substitute for the real thing. It is just the same hether you are shopping for sofas or designing them – the final test is simply what it feels like. Whenever e design a sofa or armchair, or indeed any other product, the last stage before a design goes into roduction is the full-size sample. And there is no better way of assessing what changes must be made han inviting people of all shapes and sizes to come and try out the item in question. While certain arameters are common to us all and tiny variations – adjustments of a couple of degrees in the angle of e back, ten millimetres more on the width of the arms and the final choice of the fabric – can make all e difference, comfort has to be felt to be believed.

**haped to fit the body, or padded and upholstered to provide a resilient seat for
elaxation, the truly comfortable chair is a considerable design challenge.**

touch

Cotton is exceptionally tough. The longest-staple fibres, such as Egyptian cotton, are strong enough to be woven into sailcloth. Line-drying may be time-consuming, but nothing smells better than sheets hung out in the sun and fresh air.

Touch offers creature comfort at its most basic and intimate. What we allow next to the skin – from the tips of the fingers to the soles of the feet – has an acute influence on the way we feel. The pleasure and reassurance we derive from such experiences starts at a young age. A baby nuzzles the satin binding on a 'security' blanket because it is a reminder of its mother's skin; a toddler clings to the familiar matted fur of a favourite teddy-bear; a child is hypersensitive to any clothing that is itchy or scratchy and inseparable from what is well worn and soft. Things that are nice to touch are frequently embedded with memories.

Touch can also be a performance-indicator: the honeycombed texture of waffleweave fabrics and the pile of terrycloth signal their superior absorbency; the dense weight of tightly woven wool suggests warmth.

One of the most delightful materials to touch is cashmere. Incredibly soft and featherlight, cashmere is spun from the exceptionally fine hairs of the cashmere goat, a species that lives in high, inaccessible parts of the world. The density and fineness of the animal's coat helps to trap a layer of warm air close to its skin and maintain body temperature in a cold mountain habitat. When the yarn is woven into

blankets, shawls or clothing, the result is a material that provides an almost weightless warmth. Cashmere is costly, but unlike other more spurious forms of luxury, it is not expensive simply because it is expensive: there is a good reason for the price tag. Cashmere goats could be farmed in less remote areas that entail fewer transportation costs, but there would be little point – at lower altitudes there is no need for the goat to grow its fine, insulating undercoat. Spinning yarn from such delicate fibres is a relatively difficult process which also costs more than spinning sheep's wool, for example. Cashmere will never be cheap, but it is one of those luxuries that remain well worth the investment.

Cashmere can hardly be regarded as an essential, but many people could afford to be more discriminating in their choice of other fabrics and materials around the home. Most critical to comfort is the quality of bedlinen. While you may actually handle certain types of soft furnishings, such as curtains or tablecloths, only a couple of times a day, you spend nearly a third of your life lying between sheets or under a duvet. Bedlinen made of natural fibres may be more expensive than that made of synthetics and more difficult to wash and iron but the difference in price is negligible compared to the difference in comfort. Of course, people don't buy synthetic materials simply because they are cheaper but because they promise easy care. But if you compare the small amount of extra time you might need to spend maintaining bedlinen made of pure cotton or linen with the considerable degree of pleasure they offer during hours of use, the balance weighs firmly in their favour.

From the Middle Ages to the mechanization of cotton production, bedlinen, as the name suggests, was always made of linen, as were, for that matter, tablecloths, shirts and underclothes. Linen comes from the flax plant, grown widely in northern Europe; the fibre, which comes from the inner bark, is very strong, long-lasting and hard-wearing. Like all natural materials, the woven fabric has good 'transpirational' qualities, which means that it breathes. We experience this as a coolness and dryness on the skin – linen is quick to absorb moisture and quick to dry out. Old linen sheets are even better than new ones; the fabric simply grows softer with repeated washing. Linen is comparatively expensive, as processing flax is a complex procedure; the price is also determined by the basic characteristics of the fibre, with Belgium and Ireland producing the highest quality.

More affordable, but offering almost the same degree of tactile enjoyment, is pure cotton. Like linen, cotton has an ancient pedigree, dating back to early Egyptian, Indian and Chinese civilizations. It is now grown all over the world in warm to hot climatic zones, with a significant proportion of the world's output coming from the United States. As most of us appreciate from wearing cotton clothing, it is another fabric that breathes, allowing air to circulate next to the skin and making it a cool and comfortable material for both shirts and sheets.

For those of us in northern latitudes, beds swathed in filmy drapery are purely romantic. In tropical areas, such a treatment has a practical purpose. Fine, light cotton, such as muslin, is often used as mosquito netting but it also allows air to circulate on hot, humid nights.

Textiles appeal to our sensual natures. Sumptuous fabrics such as velvet and brocade look and feel wonderful but, like leather, they can be overwhelming if used on a large scale. However, as accents – cushion covers, upholstery or throws – they bring an extra-special dimension of comfort.

Cotton is made from the fibres of the boll or fruit of the cotton plant. When the boll ripens and bursts, it frees seeds attached to fibrous tufts, tufts that are then harvested, dried, cleaned and pressed into bales for spinning. The quality of cotton is determined by the staple length, or length of the fibre. The highest quality cotton comes from long-staple fibres such as sea island and Egyptian, which can be woven into material light enough for the finest dress shirt or strong enough for the sails of a yacht. Short-staple cotton is grown mainly in Asia and results in coarser, less durable fabrics such as muslin, gingham and madras. Most cotton is woven from mid-range fibres; American cotton falls into this category. Perhaps genetic engineering will allow the staples to be lengthened.

Natural fibres, whether they are animal or vegetable in derivation, have built-in characteristics that help keep the body at an even temperature, neither too hot nor too cold. The same is true of other types of natural material used in the interior: stone floors in a hot climate or thick rugs in winter temper what would otherwise be extreme conditions and make them liveable. Synthetic products often fail spectacularly in this respect, as anyone who has spent a night sticking to or shivering between nylon sheets will testify. Feeling relaxed and easy in one's skin depends on the degree of basic comfort next to it.

On a more emotional level textiles, as one critic, Pamela Johnson of the University of East Anglia, has recently pointed out, can have a calming effect, related to the repetitive nature of the making process, whether it is weaving or knitting: 'The soothing process results in the soothing object.' Soothing is precisely the right term to describe the sensation of sliding between cool, clean cotton sheets or spreading a warm woollen blanket over your legs on a chilly night. Smoothness is also soothing – we are instinctively drawn to surfaces as soft as skin.

Fabrics can arouse passionate responses. One of those who admires the quality of different materials is Min Hogg, editor of *The World of Interiors*, who believes that fabrics epitomize 'everything that is glorious about man's ability to make something', expressing the disciplines of different techniques from industrial engineering to handmaking. Nothing gives her more pleasure than the noises fabrics make, how they feel when you touch them or the way that light falls on a crumpled piece of taffeta, for example. Just as clean sheets offer a 'frisson of pleasure', she recommends that all covers and curtains be machine-washable.

I began my career as a textile designer and in a book I once wrote about the subject I said, 'Pattern fulfils two human needs in that it can be both stimulating and tranquillizing.' For 'pattern' I could have equally substituted 'texture'; in the context

of textiles such elements are often interchangeable. An textile designer must understand how cloth is woven and th is all the more important where patterns are woven in, rathe than printed on, the surface. When we design a new rang of bedlinen, for example, the process may begin on pape but, as is the case with the prototype sofa, a key stag is translating a two-dimensional idea into somethin approximating the real thing. For a fabric designed to b woven in stripes of colour, this stage might consist of makin 'windings' where the pattern of colours is translated int alternating yarns or threads wound round a strip of foa board or card. This part of the design process supplies th dimension missing from the drawing board – that of touch.

As the terms bedclothes and bedlinen indicate, there a close relationship between the materials we wear an those with which we dress the home, which may account fo the affection they inspire. Sofa and chair upholstery can b clean-lined and tailored or loose and unstructured, while suc details as cushion covers could be seen as the fashionabl accessory of the home's wardrobe, supplying an accent c colour or contrast of texture that brings a look together. Th clothing metaphor can be taken almost literally: knitte cushion covers fastened with horn buttons are only one ste removed from the woolly jumper in your drawer. A dévore velvet throw is merely a bigger example of what you migh wrap round your shoulders. Suede trousers and suede cushions appear in the shops at the same time, sharin the same fashionable cachet. We would probably fee overwhelmed by such materials if they were used on a muc larger scale – suede or velvet covering every chair, bed an window would be sheer overkill unless you were designin a bordello – but as small 'touches' they add a sense of vitality and perhaps a hint of eroticism.

As far as touch is concerned, the surface that offers potentially the highest degree of daily contact is the floor. We walk on it, sit on it, lounge on it; it is the first surface we meet when we get out of bed or the bath; children crawl and play on it. Even with the protection of shoes, the floor can provide a textural dimension, an interest that is further developed

We are most aware of comfort next to the skin, which means that our choice of bedlinen is critical. Natural fabrics, such as cotton, linen and wool, feel and perform infinitely better than their synthetic counterparts, and are well worth the extra investment of time and money. Whether you are a devotee of the duvet or a sheet-and-blankets fan, quality matters. Immaculate detailing, such as button fastenings, adds finesse.

The way different fabrics feel
can indicate how they will
perform practically. The thick
pile of terrycloth soaks up
moisture from the skin; similarly,
the indentations in waffleweave
are what make it so absorbent.
Steer clear of poor quality towels
– they may feel dense and heavy
when you buy them, but many
have added bulking agents that
vanish at the first wash.

en different materials are combined: brick and wood, stone
d rug, slate and marble. But the visual delight offered by
xtural variety is not the same as the pleasure of touch.
poring made of natural plant fibres, such as sisal, coir and
agrass, appear full of character when you look at them,
t can be distinctly lacking in comfort: all you have to do is
k a child. However, in eastern cultures, such as that of
pan, where shoelessness is the norm indoors, and living
ditionally takes place at floor level, more attention is paid
comfort underfoot. The springiness of smooth tatami
atting made from fine reeds is both resilient enough to sit
and sleep on and kind to stockinged feet.

Walking barefoot or in stockinged feet is one of the most
laxing things you can do. Although we may keep our shoes
for most of the time in the West, it is certainly worth
oviding something enjoyable and accommodating to step
, at least in those areas where encounters between bare
et and floor take place regularly. Carpet or a rug by the side
the bed, cork or slatted wooden mats by the bath, mosaic
es in the shower stall and worn flagstones on a sunny
rrace give pleasure from the ground up.

Touch connects us with the
physical world. Natural materials
provide a variety of tactile
experiences that give pleasure
on a barely conscious level but
which are no less important for
that. The feel of cotton or linen
next to the skin, or smooth
stone, mosaic or wood
underfoot cannot be simulated.

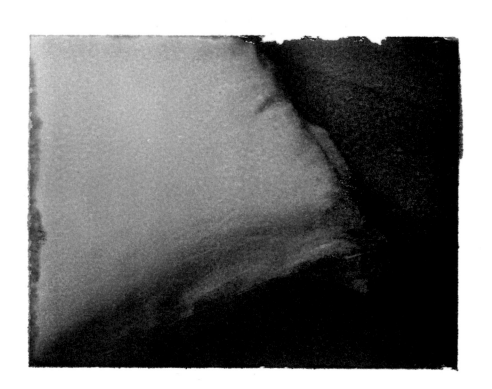

sleep

...rilyn Monroe famously wore only Chanel No 5 in hers, but ...n if you are less minimally dressed between the sheets, ...d is still the place where we are most critically aware of ...nfort or the lack of it. The fairy tale about the princess who ...s so sensitive that she could detect the presence of a ...le pea lurking under layers and layers of feather bedding ...enerally read as a parable about gentility and refinement, ...it could serve equally well as an illustration of how ...n minor shortfalls in bedroom comfort can make for nights ...oubled sleep.

Sleep deprivation, as any new parent or torturer worth ...salt could tell you, is the fastest route to mental and ...sical collapse. The body needs sleep to replenish its ...rgy reserves, to fight off illness and to rest muscles and ...ts; arguably, we also need sleep to dream, the activity ...ng which the mind beds down the experiences of the day. ...eepless night (what the French call *une nuit blanche*, or ...vhite night') often precedes a disastrous day beset by ...idents, lapses in concentration and bad temper; after a ...d night's sleep, most people are ready, both physically ...mentally, for anything. Sleep is much more than the ...nate in relaxation.

Many things can keep you awake at night – noisy ...ghbours, crying babies, snoring partners, looming ...dlines, unresolved problems – but there is no reason why ...r bed should be one of them. A decent bed is the bottom ...in night-time comfort and the most important purchase ...will ever make. A good bed can certainly be stylish, but ...e is absolutely no point in forking out huge sums on a four-...ter with all the fancy trimmings if the mattress is ...standard or the bed base is flimsy. The quality of a bed ...s in more prosaic details of construction and composition ...ch are rarely apparent at first sight but should be ...ediately obvious the minute you lie down.

If one should always try to buy the best that one can ...rd, this is doubly true when it comes to choosing a bed. ...ood bed – specifically, a good mattress – supports the ...y's weight, cushions the spine and is resilient enough to ...ommodate shifts of position without sagging.

...nfort makes the difference between sweet dreams and a restless night. The best bed and ...ttress you can afford are essential for healthy sleep and daily well-being.

People have varying tastes when it comes to the softness or hardness of beds, but in practical terms the spectrum is actually fairly narrow. If the mattress is too hard and unyielding, the body will be forced out of its natural alignment; if it is too soft, your weight will simply trap you in a fixed position for the entire night. The result, in either case, will be cramp, stiff joints and sore muscles or, worse, long-term back problems. Factor another person who may be a different height, a different weight and have a different sleeping pattern into the equation and the demands become more acute. A good mattress should not be a seesaw, always tipping down on the side bearing the most weight. It should also be covered in a durable material made of natural fibre, such as cotton ticking, to allow air to circulate and promote the absorption of moisture.

The quality of a mattress is determined primarily by the method of construction. The best and most expensive mattresses are made up of a large number of individual springs set into pockets. As the springs move independently, the mattress will give only where weight is applied, providing the optimum comfort for two people sharing a bed, especially desirable where the weights differ greatly. Another type of sprung mattress consists of a continuous network or coil of springs; the denser the springs, the better the quality. Solid foam mattresses, which are specifically designed to be used with sprung bases, also vary in thickness, comfort and, hence, quality.

hen it comes to sleeping
bits, people generally fall into
o categories: larks and owls.
t even if you like to sleep late
a darkened room, windows
e essential to allow fresh air
circulate. In Britain, at least,
oom is not deemed 'habitable'
less it has a window. Shutters
een the light almost totally
r left), **while placing the bed
that the light falls at the foot
it rather than at the top
events early morning glare
ft). A wrap-around view of sea
d sky would appeal to true
rly birds** (below).

Pillows also vary in content and quality; choose the variety that provides the best support for your neck and head. Down-filled pillows are the most expensive and softest; more resilient are feather-and-down mixtures or all-feather. Goose and duck feathers are naturally curly, giving added springiness. Synthetic fibre or foam pillows are advisable if you suffer from allergies.

Unfortunately, unlike other purchases made with an eye for quality, mattresses do not improve with time. Regular turning, from side to side and top to bottom, will help to distribute wear evenly, and regular airing is essential, but all mattresses have a finite lifespan, normally no longer than about a decade. Pillows last a much shorter time; when they become floppy and saggy, it's time for them to go.

What we sleep between is just as important as what we sleep on. As I have mentioned earlier, sheets and bedding made of natural fibres create a temperate zone next to the skin, a soothing combination of dryness, coolness and smoothness. But the body also needs warmth, which is where the duvet versus blankets debate comes in. I can take some credit for introducing the duvet to British households; we first stocked 'continental quilts' in Habitat in 1964. Since that time, the majority of this country have overcome their initial suspicions and woken up to the duvet

Bed is a private space where we can feel vulnerable; some form of enclosure, or suggestion of it, makes us feel more secure. Even in cool climates, simple drapery such as suspended netting can be very atmospheric (above). **Sunlight streams over this bed placed snugly against a window reveal** (left). **In a high-ceilinged space, the position of the bed by the staircase creates a feeling of intimacy** (right). **One of the most appealing sleeping arrangements is the box bed** (far right); **tongue-and-groove panelling and a useful ledge makes a cosy alcove.**

The trusses, beams and columns of this converted attic create natural points of demarcation between different areas.

considerable practical advantages. Warm, light and obviating the need for time-consuming bedmaking, the duvet has now all but lost the 'foreignness' of its origins to become an unremarkable household basic. Available in different densities or 'tog' ratings for varying degrees of warmth, the best duvets owe their superb insulating characteristics to real feathers and/or down rather than synthetic fibres. Tastes are notoriously fickle, however, and along with the ubiquity of the duvet has come a renewed affection for old-fashioned sheets and blankets among the fashion-conscious or those lucky enough to have somebody to make the bed for them – this is perhaps the result of perceived, rather than actual, comfort.

Bed, however, is more than a comfortable place to sleep. As the duvet/blanket divide reveals, a certain sense of nostalgia can have more than a part to play. Bed is the ultimate personal domain; in fact, it is our first private space. The attachment most children feel to their own beds, despite their disinclination to go to sleep, is profoundly territorial and this sense of refuge or nesting instinct lingers on into adulthood. Whether we huddle under the duvet, or draw up the blankets, bed offers psychological and emotional comfort as well as the merely physical. This may be why eating in bed, reading in bed, thinking in bed and even working in bed can seem such pleasant indulgences.

This broader dimension of comfort can be enhanced – or undermined – by the way you arrange, furnish and light the bedroom. The bedroom, which, like the bathroom, is defined by its dominant piece of furniture, tends to persist even in the most determinedly open-plan living spaces. Enclosure and physical separation from other activities not only provide the privacy we desire for intimate moments, but also offer a sense of security when we feel at our most vulnerable.

Where you place the bed is a critical factor. Feng shui, as ever, has an answer for this, which is that the bed should be placed with the head against a wall to ensure solidity, stability and security, and facing the door or entrance but not directly lined up with it (in feng shui terms, a bed directly facing an open doorway is little better than a coffin ready to be carted down the stairs). More prosaically, it makes sense to position the bed so that there is plenty of clear space surrounding it, to avoid the low-level frustration that results when bedmaking becomes an obstacle course and to give each side of the bed equal ease of access.

We no longer need heavy bed drapery to provide warmth, but even light fabric can offer a sense of enclosure.

Naturally, feng shui also has a great deal to say on the subject of orientation, that is which point of the compass the bed should face. South is recommended for fame, north for success in business, east for a happy family life, and so on. (It's not clear what you should do if you want to achieve all these aims – place the bed on a revolving pedestal, perhaps.) We might find the issue of orientation more relevant in terms of the quality of light. A room facing east, for example, catches the early morning sun; dawn light provides a gentler and more natural way of waking up than a buzzing alarm clock.

Light control is much more important in bedrooms than might first be imagined, given that a large proportion of the time we spend there is during the hours of darkness. In urban areas, however, the spill of light from streetlamps means that darkness is rarely total, and some form of screening is essential. On the other hand, morning light creates an inherent mood of optimism, so a complete blackout is usually

a bad idea. Curtains or blinds that filter the light rather than block it out entirely strike a balance. As far as artificial lighting is concerned, it is crucial to avoid overhead glare from a central fixture; if such an arrangement is harsh in a living area, it is twice as uncomfortable when your principal viewpoint is from a supine position. In a similar way, bedrooms benefit from good ventilation; fresh air is just as important as the right lighting in creating revitalizing and restful conditions. Deadening sound can also be an important consideration, especially if you live in a busy urban area, but even a cock crowing in the country can wake you earlier than you wish.

A comfortable bed, subtle light and gentle airflow provide the basic ingredients for peaceful sleep – and for those key transitory times when we unwind and wake up. But the bedroom, despite its name, often gathers in a variety of other functions and their accompanying paraphernalia – activities that can erode the contemplative mood.

Le Corbusier, who we have to remember was Swiss, had strong opinions on this subject as on many others; he well known for denouncing the habit of keeping clothes in the bedroom, a practice he regarded as unsanitary. His view may display a rather zealous attitude to personal hygiene but it does hint at the potential for conflict. While I doubt that dressing in the bedroom poses a significant risk to one' health, it does entail turning a large portion of the availabl space over to storage. Traditional pieces of storage furniture such as wardrobes and chests of drawers, devour space an serve as additional navigational obstacles in a room wher the bed already takes up a considerable amount of floor are. Open storage systems, such as clothes rails and fitte shelving may be physically less intrusive but the overall effec can be rather like sleeping in a shop. If you are going to shar your sleeping space with your entire wardrobe, it make sense to construct closets and other concealed forms o

storage that provide an uninterrupted background. Better still, borrow space from somewhere else – a landing, bathroom or hallway – and build a dressing area where you can organize your clothes systematically.

Min Hogg has recently put one of her 'room theories' into practice, turning what had formerly been, at various times, a dining room and a spare room into a dressing room. What might at first seem a dramatic, almost wilful, sacrifice of space has had an entirely beneficial effect: the change it has made to her life is 'a joy', she says. Her clothes, bags, shoes and scarves are still housed all in one place, but she can now shut the door on them, and if they become disorganized, it takes only a matter of seconds to get them back into what she considers to be good order. However, the greatest advantage she has discovered is that by moving her 'clutter and clobber' elsewhere, the bedroom has been released into a more 'living' room.

Attention to detail – the accent of colour, the right level of lighting, places to put things such as glasses of water and books – is as important In the bedroom as anywhere else.

bathe

Water is undoubtedly therapeutic, the directness of contact being part of the pleasure. This minimal shower (far right), designed by Claudio Silvestrin, is little more than a water jet set into a panel of stone, which reduces bathing to the bare essentials.

Bathing, for all its virtuous connotations, is less about function than pleasure and comfort. Few of us nowadays, in our machine-washed, dry-cleaned clothes and white-collar jobs, get as visibly dirty as we would have done in previous centuries working on the land or at some other form of heavy manual labour. Just as the advent of domestic appliances, such as the vacuum cleaner, increased our expectations of how clean a home could be, indoor plumbing, dependable drainage and endless hot water have extended our standards of personal hygiene. It has never been easier to keep clean, but scrubbing off the grime of a hard day's toil at a computer terminal must realistically rank second in importance to the sheer sensual bliss of a hot soak or the mental invigoration of a shower. Today, most of us bathe primarily to wash away our cares; keeping clean goes without saying.

Water has a powerful appeal. From sea-bathing to skinny-dipping or simply messing around in boats, it provides a focus for countless holidays. You might trace the fascination to our ancestors' supposed origins in the primeval oceans, or no further back than the womb, but water is a medium that feels both instinctively pleasurable and utterly therapeutic.

It is odd, then, when we have regularly gone to considerable lengths to seek out spas, seasides and water resorts, that the bathroom, which offers immediate access to similarly elemental delights, has often been one of the least satisfactory areas in the home. Until fairly recently, cold, clinical and cramped would have been a fair description of many British bathrooms, the meanness of the aesthetic reflecting, perhaps, a coyness about bodily functions, coupled with a certain puritanical suspicion of well-being – not surprising, I suppose, in a race brought up to believe in the moral value of the cold shower. There are, however, encouraging signs that a certain reassessment is underway. The change in attitude, like many shifts in the way we view our homes, has gone hand in hand with an increased exposure to the wider world.

I can vividly remember the experience of bathing in a hotel in the Italian resort of Positano. The bathroom window looked out over the sea, which was pleasant enough, but the lower portion of the window was fashioned into a glazed fish tank. From one's eyeline, then, sitting in the tub, there was this incredibly watery view, with the fish in the tank merging almost seamlessly with the blue sea beyond. In terms of capturing the mood of the setting, the effect far surpassed the desultory collection of seashells or display of beachcombing relics that seem to be the more typical expressions of seaside inspiration.

That experience was unique and specific. Other inspirational influences may come from contact with the bathing customs of different cultures. The Scandinavian sauna, Turkish steam bath, Japanese jacuzzi or Californian hot tub display very different approaches to relaxing and/or keeping clean, but their common denominator is a certain uninhibited, if not to say communal, enjoyment of water, steam or heat. Although it is not necessary and, indeed, for many people it may be prohibitively expensive or impractical to install the required fixtures and fittings in the home, the basic attitude is well worth emulating.

The pleasures of bathing are enhanced when the setting provides a link with the outside world. In a warm climate, fresh breezes through open doorways and a tantalizing garden view are the next best thing to showering outdoors – and the antithesis of a cramped cell-like space with its punitive overtones.

The first step, surely, must be to create surroundings that are pleasant to spend time in. The challenge is to do so within very real, practical constraints. The clinical bathroom, with its tetchy undercurrent of anxiety about germs and smells, is often a repellent place where no one would wish to linger, but its laboratory-style functionalism is at least easy to maintain in a pristine state. At the opposite extreme, bathrooms furnished and fitted rather like shrunken drawing rooms are ultimately intolerant of the activities that must take place there: sodden carpet, persistent odours, mildew and damp-stained walls do not add up to an easy environment. And dressed-up, formal bathrooms can seem rather peculiar surroundings for an activity that requires you to be naked.

Somewhere between these two extremes are bathrooms whose design is founded on the display of a sympathetic mix of materials. Combinations of stone, mosaic, ceramics, glass, metal or tongue-and-groove boarding perform well on a functional level and invite our continuing interest in their evocative textural contrasts, an interest that is only heightened in a state of undress. Bathrooms where materials speak for themselves offer a way of getting back to basics – surely one of the main attractions of bathing.

As far as planning is concerned, be as generous with space as you can: think of the delightfully pampering quality of a bathroom in a good hotel. A big bathroom and a big bath lift the spirits and liberate the mind for creative daydreaming, which is another one of the pleasures of bathing. Equally important, a larger area permits flexibility of layout, so the bath can be positioned in a freer arrangement, either with just its head against the wall or pulled away from the wall entirely and aligned to take advantage of a view. A greater degree of space allows a more congenial segregation of activities than a confined bathroom, which can often be fitted out in only one way, with lavatory, bath and washbasin in a tight grouping that is as constricting physically as it is psychologically. A big bathroom also means that there is space in between these necessary fixtures for other pieces of furniture, such as chests, chairs or free-standing shelves, which can make a bathroom so hospitable. But if your spatial

If the bathroom is spacious, it can often be a good idea to position the bath tub so that it projects out from the wall, leaving free space on three sides. Views are equally important, as are windows that open to admit light and air, even a patch of warming sunshine.

options are very limited, remember that even a small amount of extra floor area can make a difference when it comes to juggling the planning. A doorway pulled out into a hallway by a matter of inches can give you just enough extra elbow room at a basin, for example, to make the layout workable.

'Sanitaryware', that unlovely trade term, sums up the whole no-nonsense style of standardized bathroom fittings, whose basic form has altered very little in the century or so since the demise of Thomas Crapper, the Victorian Emperor of the Bog. There's nothing wrong with such fittings, provided they are of decent quality and size – and, of course, provided they are white – but aesthetically they offer little more than the comfort of the expected. More recently, new designs have emerged that take a more playful, sculptural approach to the whole issue. Cantilevered basins in glass or metal, sinks that defiantly expose the working plumbing, tubs that are sleek and streamlined or big-bellied and free-standing run the full stylistic gamut from minimal to expressive, while at the technological cutting edge, showers or taps lit fibre-optically turn running water into a theatrical play of light; there are even Japanese lavatories that wash your bottom with warm water and dry it with jets of air. An unusual location can be enough to create a provocative sense of surprise – a bath sunk flush with the floor, for example.

One of the most luxurious bathrooms in fiction is described in F. Scott Fitzgerald's story 'The Diamond As Big As The Ritz'. It, too, features a sunken bath, into which the main character, John T. Unger, is propelled by a tilting bed via a fleecy incline into an adjoining bath chamber: '. . . lining the walls of the room and the sides and bottom of the bath itself was a blue aquarium, and gazing through the crystal surface on which he sat, he could see fish swimming among amber lights and even gliding without curiosity past his outstretched toes . . . .' The sensual ambience is heightened by fountains that disperse hot rosewater, paddle-wheels that churn up a frothy foam, a 'moving-picture machine' and ambient flutes 'dripping a melody that was like a waterfall'. Unger's bath ends with a cold salt-water shower and a massage with 'oil, alcohol and spice'.

The luxury of this imagined bathtime rests in having everything done for you. A slightly more practical solution was designed by Le Corbusier for the family of some friends

Wet skin loses heat rapidly; thick, generous towels and mats to soak up the moisture are a vital part of bathroom comfort.

The water chute at Ahmadabad, India, designed by Le Corbusier, connects the summer sleeping platform on the roof of the house to the garden pool (preceding pages).

of mine at Ahmadabad in India. He had been commissioned by the parents to build a house and asked the two boys how they dreamed they might bathe in the morning. They said they would like to roll out of bed into a large, cool pool. Corbusier's solution was to construct a long terrazzo slide, lubricated with the constant trickle of water, running from the summer sleeping platform on the roof into the pool in the garden below. It is the perfect way to begin the day in the heat of India.

In Philippe Starck's recent bathroom designs, based on the archetypal container shapes of the bucket and trough, the aim is neither to overturn convention nor induce a sense of pampered luxury. Instead, it is to reacquaint us with a directness of experience and remind us of those simple acts such as stooping down to cup water from a pool or pouring a jug of water over one's body – similar to those

unsophisticated, unselfconscious moments of intimacy seen in the paintings of Degas and Bonnard. The basic premise is, perhaps, that plumbing, by delivering water on tap, has somehow managed to distance us from the true feeling of spontaneity that bathing can offer.

As with sleeping, bathing is an activity where comfort is as critical before and after it takes place as it is during the event. Towels or robes warmed on a heated rail, non-slip surfaces underfoot, generous towels to absorb water from your body are just as integral to a comfortable bath as the right water temperature. Wet skin quickly becomes cold and is more susceptible to abrasion from rough textures, which is why the quality of bath towels and flannels is important. Terrycloth is not as absorbent as commonly supposed, especially if it has been given a velvet finish;

A bathroom in a converted Brussels shop offers a charming departure from the expected (above): **the sink plumbed into an old free-standing cupboard, metal boxes and trunks for storage and a claw-foot bath.**

any bathrooms and cloakrooms are necessarily small; a wall covered in mirror multiplies the sense of space (right). A room with a view: this low-level bath sunk into the floor and screened by blinds and curtains is the perfect spot for daydreaming (below).

waffleweave fabrics soak up water much more readily. Cheap towels, even those that give every impression of softness, have often been treated with chemicals to improve the way they feel, a temporary finish that can increase water-resistance. After a few washes, however, a poor quality product will be all too obvious.

The bathroom has traditionally been the focus for much spurious luxury, with coloured suites, mahogany loo seats, gilt taps and ostentatious brass-plated shower sets. At the same time, the Victorian notion of 'cleanliness is next to godliness' has taken quite a mystic turn during recent years, with bathside candles and aromatherapy oils elevating the entire bathing experience to a kind of high communion. I'm all for the sybaritic pleasures of fine soaps and scents but, for me, the real luxury of bathing remains its easy simplicity.

function

Easy living demands a home that works as well as it looks. Things that function properly and suit the task for which they are required, a basic infrastructure that is accommodating and well planned, and a natural sense of order smooth your path. Easy living, of course, could mean getting someone else to do all the work for you, but as a person who actually enjoys what he does, I prefer to think of it as a way of ensuring that work itself is a pleasure.

Splitting life down the middle, with chores in one half and fun in the other, seems profoundly unsatisfactory to me. Real pleasure goes hand in hand with practicality: a kitchen that is functional will also be a place of creative satisfaction; knives, forks and glasses that perform the way they should and look good will add joy to the experience of eating and drinking. Drudgery – which we're all keen to avoid – is not merely monotonous physical effort but a relentless uphill struggle where things are constantly breaking, failing or getting lost and materials are just not up to scratch.

Throughout this century, mechanization has been seen as the universal answer to the problem of work. But turning to technology as a fail-safe way of making life easier can be a Faustian pact. Everyone is familiar with the household gadget that takes longer to find, assemble, operate, clean and put away again than the procedure it is designed to perform. Such 'labour-saving' devices only save labour in the narrowest sense when the button is pressed or switch is flicked; in the wider scheme of things they can be irritating, time-consuming and difficult to use and maintain. Of course, I am not suggesting that one should turn the clock back, replace vacuum cleaners with carpet beaters or scrub the sheets by hand, but there are many situations when a simple, direct approach remains the easiest and most enjoyable of all. A good, sharp knife, for example, functions far more efficiently in ordinary circumstances than the most heavily accessorized food processor, and when it 'fails', you simply have to sharpen it, not reread the instruction manual, hunt for the lost part, check the guarantee or phone the supplier – only to be told that the model is now out of production and cannot be repaired.

Technology, which is supposed to be our helpmate, can often leave us helpless. An amusing story recently appeared in the papers about Bill Gates' first night in his new 'smart' house. A large television screen, programmed to slide in and out of a console on demand, refused either to retract or turn off. Unfortunately, the screen was located in the bedroom and, in the interests of a decent night's sleep, the only solution was to throw a blanket over it. No doubt we will be throwing blankets over many technological gizmos on 1st January 2000, at one minute past midnight.

Anyone who has ever been driven into a blind fury by a non-functioning piece of equipment whose breakdown is as total as it is mysterious will recognize the frustration. My own central heating system is so intelligent that when it goes wrong I have no access to it or way of coping with it; my only recourse is to ring the service engineers. Such situations bring to mind a comment once made by the president of the French booksellers' association. Faced with the failure of a complex audiovisual presentation, he reminded those of us in the audience that 'books don't break'. In this sense,

technology can also be distancing, replacing a directness of experience and control with something that requires the expert intervention of third parties. It seems to me that one of the components of an easy life is to surround yourself only with well-proven technology; the cutting edge can damage your life.

Rather than investing in technology that will end up running the show or dominating all your waking hours, I believe it is better to spend time thinking about what you really need and the way you like to live. On one level, everyone needs the basic degree of practicality where services are well integrated, pipes and wires are hidden, controls are properly positioned and taps do not drip or leak. But on another level, what makes your home function properly and your life easier may be very different from the type of surroundings that work for others. Min Hogg, for example, insists on keeping a pair of scissors in every room, despite the fact that she lives in an apartment and not a rambling house on several levels. For others, it may be always having pen and paper close to hand or never being far from a socket for plugging in the laptop computer . . . easy living rests on the fundamental principle of suiting yourself.

order

Life attracts clutter as surely as a letterbox attracts junk mail. You may begin with a relatively clean slate but within a terrifying short space of time find yourself sharing your home with a morass of irrelevant detail: gadgets you never use, instruction manuals for gadgets you no longer own, unwelcome gifts and wedding presents, clothes that don't fit or suit you, spare parts for machines you have long since upgraded, half-consumed packets of foodstuffs you don't like, books that don't bear a second reading and, worse, books that, if you are honest with yourself, you are never going to read in the first place.

It is not particularly difficult to identify what is redundant baggage, nor is it hard to get rid of it. In many cases, all it takes is a little ruthlessness and a few spare moments; at the most painful, you should need only the relatively small degree of courage that is required to look the bad bargain or false economy straight in the eye and discard it, sadder but certainly wiser.

On this level, good order is merely common sense. Time is one of the most valuable commodities we have and if you are one of those people who seems to spend ninety per cent of their waking hours looking for things, sparing an hour or two for a clearout is the single most important step you can take towards improving your life. Clutter in this sense is simply a waste of energy, where ordinary routines are unnecessarily complicated, and there is the constant feeling of working in your own shadow. Clutter can also be expensive: plenty of people who regularly find themselves turning the house upside down looking for some essential tool or ingredient wind up buying another in sheer desperation.

But, as most people soon come to realize, the whole issue is not quite as simple as that. Personal taste also plays a part. Some people, myself included, are incredibly refreshed by simplicity – whether a clear desk, a clear floor or the sense of spaciousness and expansion that results when every available surface is not weighted down with its own cargo of belongings. Others seem to need their possessions more visibly around them, within easy, familiar reach. The expression of such nesting instincts, although they may result in environments that would cause a minimalist to recoil with horror, constitutes a very real part of what gives some of us pleasure in our own surroundings.

While I naturally subscribe to the 'fewer and better' school of thinking, I would hate everything to be under rigid control, regimented behind the closed doors of seamlessly built-in cupboards. It isn't easy living when you daren't leave newspapers strewn across the floor or an open book by the bedside: in such uptight interiors, living itself seems an intrusion. I might enjoy the uplifting sight of a clear desk, but I also take a certain pleasure from the creative messiness that is the natural by-product of work. Francis Bacon worked in the untidiest space imaginable, but produced some of the finest paintings of the twentieth century.

The principle is the same, although the aesthetic is different. Storage basically consists of variations on very simple themes: shelving, hanging and containing.

If order is to some extent in the eye of the beholder, occupying a variable position somewhere in the long continuum between minimalism and chaos, it also requires daily compromise in most households. Just as there are couples where one partner is always early and the other always late, the person who always knows where the scissors are often finds themselves sharing their life with someone who hasn't seen the bottom of their sock drawer since 1987. From the two-year-old's continual emptying of drawers, cupboards and toy boxes in the spirit of playful enquiry, to the unrivalled squalor of the teenage bedroom, children are a different matter entirely.

Living with someone who has diametrically opposed views on order can be far from easy, but it is nevertheless a challenge most of us can manage to meet. Joseph, for example, is more of a minimalist than his wife Isabel, who likes a softer look. He believes, however, that 'it is important to bring the personalities of two people together'. Suzie Slesin, on the other hand, is a self-confessed accumulator, whose work as a magazine design editor and author of numerous

Tolerance for clutter varies widely from person to person. For those who prefer very little on view, discreet storage is particularly important. In this **clutter-free zone** (above left), **cupboards built into a low-level plinth provide efficient stowing places for everyday belongings.** Storage that forms an integral part of the architecture of a space can be particularly satisfying. Shelves fitted around a door or within a tall alcove (above and left) **read as a structural element, not as an afterthought. Ron Arad's 'Bookworm'** (right) **turns storage into something altogether more playful and sculptural.**

books on style presents her with many opportunities to travel and acquire the objects of her current passions. Inevitably, her husband would prefer to live with the bare minimum. Pressure of space in their New York apartment has meant that he has had to forgo his dream of a separate clothes closet; in turn, she has stopped going to flea markets and is in what she calls a 'deacquisition phase'. Her dilemma, common to everybody who loves and is inspired by things, is that the more you buy or collect, the less space you have left to appreciate them.

It is a dilemma I have felt myself. In the living room of my house in the country, I have tried to resolve this by displaying lots of things that please me at one end of the room but keeping the other end relatively empty, so you can sit in one half and look at the other without feeling overwhelmed by clutter. Joseph, who is equally beguiled by possessions, has learned 'to appreciate things in other places rather than mine'. With communications so advanced and with so many images in books and magazines, he believes that 'it is silly to try to have everything one likes'.

What is even more important than working out a compromise is recognizing what your own tastes are in the first place. In Suzie Slesin's view, accepting who you are and what you like is the basis for easy living. 'I would love to have a plain, empty bedroom,' she says, 'but when I'm in bed I like to have a stack of magazines and books nearby and I like to be able to see photographs of my children. That means I have to provide a place to put these things.' Knowing how you like to live is fundamental to creating a home that has a truly workable sense of order, which is, after all, the only sort that counts.

Given our varying attitudes to clutter and order, there are nevertheless some strategies everyone can profit by. The first, as already discussed, is to get rid of what is redundant and meaningless. You may like a lot of things around you, but there is no good reason why such items should be ugly, useless or past their sell-by date. The second is to provide sensible homes for what you do decide to keep. There is a real pleasure in what Min Hogg calls 'stowing', finding good practical places to keep things. Even children, for all their chaotic disorganization, instinctively appreciate the appeal of squirrelling things away. The childhood 'treasure' box, filled with arcane collections of meaningful bits and pieces is essentially, as one critic has said, a 'portable, tangible secret'. The pleasure of stowing owes something to this feeling, as well as the sense of resourcefulness that comes when cupboards are well stocked and shipshape.

Storage conceived as part of the overall visual effect of the room and designed to fit what is being stored is profoundly satisfying. In Min's case, two sides of her kitchen are fitted with shelves at the upper level – a narrow one for glasses so that they can be arranged only two deep, and a wider one that takes plates, stacked one pile deep. The array of glasses and plates forms an intrinsic part of the room's look.

Equally important, however, is that everything is accessible and nothing is shoved to the back of a cupboard where it won't be noticed or get used. Accessibility, in its wider sense, also means arranging your possessions so that you take some account of how often you will need them. Daily use means right at hand; once a year at Christmas means stored out of the way in the loft.

Some of the most appealing 'stowing' places are storage rooms. The dressing room, larder, workshop, shed or garage, with belongings neatly organized and in one place, may initially seem like a sacrifice of space, but can vastly improve the way that surrounding living areas work. Similarly, wide hallways lined with bookshelves or cupboards can be both extremely hard-working and full of architectural character. I particularly enjoy the ingenuity of small fitted spaces: the lockers of a ship's cabin or the detailing of old Pullman coaches on trains can be an inspiration for home storage.

All types of storage consist of variations on very simple themes: containing (in cupboards, drawers, baskets or boxes), hanging (from rails, racks, pegs or hooks) or shelving. Such basic formats have an inherent versatility, which is part of their appeal and their practicality. A wire-mesh trolley, for example, could provide storage for home office supplies, cosmetics, toys or vegetables. In the same way, the borrowing of storage fittings and furniture from retail and commercial sectors is an expression of their inherent flexibility as much as an appreciation of their looks.

Storage can be less satisfactory, however, when it involves specific accessories, such as plastic pocketed shoe 'tidies' or drawer inserts for segregating every pair of pants or socks. Such forms of organization can be irritating and fiddly to use; rather than streamlining your belongings, they simply introduce another level of clutter. A classic example of this appeared recently in a mail-order catalogue in the form of a 'stair basket'. This shaped wicker container was designed to provide a home for all those items that collect at the bottom of the stairs, awaiting relocation to rooms on the next floor up. In many homes, certain belongings do hover about in transit from time to time, but if your staircase has become a regular dumping ground, a much better solution would surely be to work out why this keeps happening – for example, are the items in question being stored too far away from where they are being used? – than to buy something that simply contributes to the clutter.

To be workable, all systems should be personal to some degree. Order is merely a way of arranging things so that they can be used in the most effective way; this is why you do not find tins and jars organized alphabetically in most kitchen cupboards. Storage systems, from fitted kitchen units to flat-pack bookshelves, offer standardized modules of space that often require customization to be of any use at all.

Some of the best storage solutions are often the simplest; peg rails and coat hooks keep outdoor gear accessible and orderly. This slightly more eccentric version has 'pegs' made from beachstones tied on to a pole with twine (above). **Hand and bath towels hanging on a plain wooden rail or suits neatly lined up along a metal, shop-style fitting are arrangements that look good as well as being practical.**

Keeping possessions behind
closed doors is one solution
to the problem of order. Floor-
to-ceiling cupboards provide
integrated, seamless storage,
but visual pleasure can also be
derived from organized display,
whether behind glazed doors,
in open units or on shelves.

With units, this might entail interior shelves spaced at different intervals and of different depths, or pull-out trays or baskets. With shelving, adjustment should be possible to accommodate the different heights, weights and sizes of books.

Order may mean clearing out everything surplus to requirements or, as in the case of Min Hogg's scissors, having a surplus of some items so they are always to hand. Equally, it can rest simply in those lateral inspirations that keep life running smoothly. Min keeps a large notebook beside the telephone, where she can note down the sort of minor domestic detail (the boiler mender's phone number and so on) that tends to get scribbled on scraps of paper and promptly lost. She dates the page and files the notebooks once they are filled – a small practicality that saves time and duplicated effort. But the value of the exercise is not merely practical; the notebooks are bound in red velvet, offering daily pleasure on this little level.

cook

Elizabeth David's 'summer' kitchen (far right), at the rear of her house in Chelsea, is the working room where she tried out dishes and wrote up recipes for her books. Plates are racked and utensils hung within easy reach – everything accessible and nothing for show. Simple and unpretentious, there is nothing haphazard about the arrangement or fitting out of this thinking and working space.

'An omelette and a salad and a piece of cheese . . . we won't make any fuss, but what we will have will be well chosen, and go nicely with a glass of wine,' wrote Elizabeth David. Her passion for flavour, simplicity and the freshest of ingredients, conveyed in lyrical prose, transformed the way we cook.

I can well remember the impact of *A Book of Mediterranean Food*, published in 1950 after a miserable decade of belt-tightening and rationing. Roughly coinciding with my own first exposure to France, the book presented a tantalizing glimpse of a culture where cooking was an art (in fact, it is the tenth art in France) and a pleasure, not a dull chore whose sole purpose was to keep body and soul together.

Reading her description of a Venetian market, one can almost taste the food: '. . . the cabbages are cobalt blue, the beetroots deep rose, the lettuces pure clear green, sharp as glass. Bunches of gaudy marrow flowers show off the elegance of pink and white marbled bean pods, primrose potatoes, green plums, green peas. The colours of the peaches, cherries and apricots, packed in boxes lined with sugar bag blue paper matching the trousers of the men unloading the gondolas are reflected in the rose-red mullet and the orange vongole . . . even ordinary sole, and ugly great skate are striped with delicate lilac lights, the sardines shine like newly minted coins . . . .' (*Italian Food*, 1954). If the sensuality of Elizabeth David's writing was intoxicating in grey, postwar Britain, the directness and 'hands-on' quality of her approach to cooking was like a breath of fresh air.

Today, our culinary horizons seem to broaden year by year. All you need do is compare the produce on supermarket shelves now with the limited range that was stocked ten, fifteen, twenty years ago – in Britain, at least, it has not been that long since the days when virtually the only place you could buy olive oil was in a chemists'. But, at the same time, all research studies agree that we are doing less and less in the kitchen. Many people's idea of making a simple meal – heating a ready-made dinner or, even worse, settling down to a takeaway on a tray in front of the television – is as far removed from Elizabeth David's omelette, salad and cheese as it is possible to be. In terms of a 'hands-on' quality, pressing buttons on the microwave or telephone is about the limit of it.

I cannot argue that real cooking involves less effort, or that it is 'easier' in the narrowest sense of the word. But I do believe that the essence of easy living sometimes resides in the ability to take the longer view, to weigh the instant convenience of a prepared packet against the satisfaction of making a truly simple meal and finding the balance tips in favour of the more authentic experience. My kind of easy cooking – the type of food that requires a slow, unattended simmering for hours, or the sort that is prepared very quickly and slung on a hot grill – does not take up very much more active time or effort, but it is infinitely more rewarding, nourishing aspects of oneself other than the physical.

What real easy cooking offers is an immediacy of experience: 'Cook and serve! Cook and serve!', as the Greek chef I hired for Cantina, one of my restaurants at Butlers Wharf, used to say. He was referring to the type of direct approach you find in the Mediterranean trattoria or taverna, where the customer is often invited to the kitchen to inspect and appreciate the freshness of the ingredients before the food is quickly cooked and delivered unceremoniously to the table. The insight is that cooking does not have to be about pretension, fiddly sauces or elaborate presentation: the 'leap in the mouth' can be the result of the most straightforward of methods – fresh, good quality ingredients simply cooked to allow the flavour to work its magic.

It is a view shared by the chef John Torode. He dislikes 'overcomplicated' food, and believes it is better to focus on one thing at a time, whatever is good and in season. 'Therefore you don't really need a lot of equipment,' he says. 'Sometimes I think we over-clutter ourselves and make things too complex; cooking becomes confused and what ends up on the plate becomes confused as well. Then when you sit down to eat, you don't really enjoy it. Whereas if you can throw something in a wok and fry it quickly, and even eat with a pair of chopsticks, it's great – and there is little washing up.'

This style of cooking goes hand in hand with a kitchen that is generous in scale, carefully planned and thoughtfully equipped. Food is one of the central pleasures of life and the kitchen should express that passion; it is even better when there is room for the enthusiasm to be shared with family and friends. When the kitchen is opened out to living and eating areas or when it is simply a big enough space in its own right, the life of the household gains a hospitable, vibrant focus, a heart of activity that keeps everything ticking over happily. I believe that kitchens that are cut off from the rest of the home, where the cook must work in isolation, often result in cooking being viewed as a chore.

This sense of inclusion does not mean, however, that you can afford to be sloppy when it comes to kitchen planning. The working areas of the kitchen, where activity is concentrated, need to be ergonomically planned to function effectively. Distances between the sink, hob, oven and fridge should not be too great: a kitchen where you can ballroom dance between counter and stove or between sink and oven is an inefficient and tiring place to work. Efficient planning makes it easier to clean up as you go along and thus avoid having to confront a daunting pile of dirty pots, pans and utensils when you have finished preparing the meal.

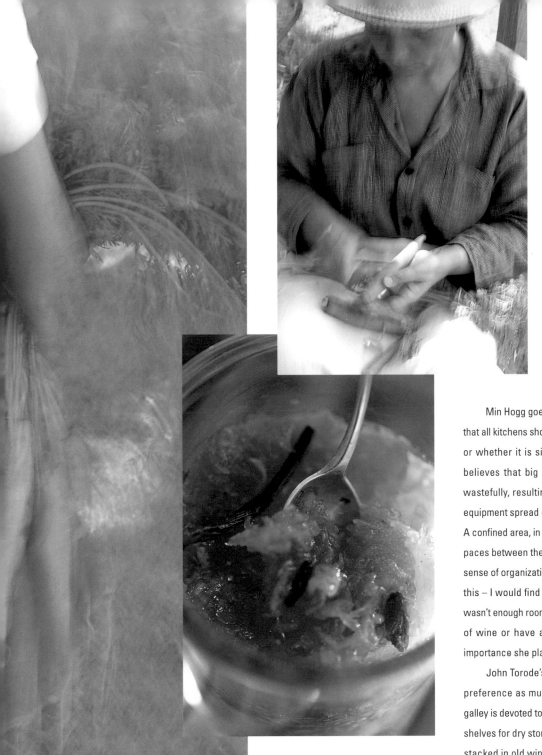

Good cooking starts with the sourcing of ingredients – the inspiration that comes from the sight, smell and feel of fresh and seasonal food. Shopping in markets or small local shops or, even better, growing your own, is more likely to get the creative juices flowing than the relentless drudgery of the weekly trip to the supermarket.

Min Hogg goes one step further in her recommendation that all kitchens should be small, no matter how big the house or whether it is situated in the town or the country. She believes that big kitchens encourage space to be used wastefully, resulting in acres of unnecessary worktop and equipment spread out from one end of the room to the other. A confined area, in her view, where there is no more than two paces between the sink, stove and fridge, promotes a better sense of organization. I can't say that I entirely go along with this – I would find it hard to work in a kitchen where there wasn't enough room for other people to join me, share a glass of wine or have a chat – but I certainly agree with the importance she places on tight planning.

John Torode's galley kitchen at home is also small, by preference as much as by circumstance. One side of the galley is devoted to a fridge, sink and stove, in that order, with shelves for dry stores at high level. Cookbooks and wine are stacked in old wine boxes and a butcher's block stands in one corner. Small spaces streamline activity and impose a certain discipline. He enjoys the feeling of being able to turn round and pick what he wants from the shelves while he is cooking or preparing food, and when cupboards and shelves become cluttered, it's time to 'throw out or stop buying'.

The restaurant kitchen is one of the most rigorous[ly] planned of all working spaces and we can learn a great de[al] from its organization. There are fewer environments whe[re] the conditions are more extreme: intense heat, sha[rp] implements and the incredible bustle of people intent on fill[ing] orders in the shortest possible time mean that precisi[on] planning is required to avoid potential disaster. In a we[ll] planned restaurant kitchen, the layout of services a[nd] appliances is firmly based on the logic of working sequenc[e] and all necessary equipment is closely integrated with t[he] preparation areas where they will be used.

The kitchen in your home is unlikely to see such [a] ferment of activity, but it is only common sense to arran[ge] fittings and fixtures so that they follow a natural progressi[on]. You should be able to move from fridge to sink to preparati[on] area to stove without too much in the way of backtrackir[g]; staple ingredients and frequently used equipment should [be] readily to hand, easily accessible and preferably in vie[w].

I am no Luddite but I do believe that most machines and gadgets have very little place in the domestic kitchen, where good, sharp knives and a skilled pair of hands can perform the majority of tasks infinitely better and quicker. Chefs are passionate about their knives; every cook should invest in the best they can afford and keep them sharpened and properly stored in a rack or block.

Cooking in a kitchen that has been properly planned sho
be a little like driving a car; you should be able to reach
the salt or a spoon as instinctively as you would engage t
clutch before changing gear.

Restaurant kitchens have had another impact on t
way we live, which is the increasing trend for profession
catering appliances and equipment to be bought for the hom
Anyone who seriously enjoys cooking is bound to apprecia
good, robust equipment that is capable of withstanding hea
use and is designed to the highest performance standar
At the same time, a vast *batterie de cuisine*, no matter h
professional it is, will not make you a better cook. I wou
agree with Elizabeth David that 'too much equipment
if anything, worse than too little', and can be the tell-tale si
of pretentiousness rather than culinary expertise.

According to John Torode, 'the easiest way to cook
to get yourself a wok and a cleaver and away you go.' Aft
all, you can fry, boil and steam in a wok and a cleaver is ju
as good at dicing shallots as it is at cracking crabs. Like
chefs, he has acquired his fair share of kitchen gadgets a
machines, often as presents, but they are rarely used. Wh
does get used, however, is equipment that is directly relat
to his particular style of cooking. For example, he has s
pestle and mortars, each with different abrasive qualitie
these include a marble one for grinding peppercorns and s
crystals, a large granite one for making curry pastes, o
used solely for grinding up turmeric and a thin, deep wood
one for pounding away at dry spices.

If people have a tendency to succumb to catering stat
symbols, they are also often seduced by 'quick-fix' kitch
gadgets. From the nifty little items that promise to halve t
time and effort taken to chop carrots to the expensive, heav
accessorized machines that really only come into their ow
when a dozen people are expected for supper, gadgets a
rarely truly necessary if you have a good range of utens
and cookware. It is far better to invest your money in hi
quality, sharp knives, heavy-gauge stainless-steel saucepa
and cast-iron casseroles that will provide years and years
dependable use. Nothing beats the humble wooden spoo

Who needs packet food when there are so many ways of cooking that are fast and simple? Stir-frying over a high heat in a wok is one of the quickest and most direct methods, and can be adapted for any number of different ingredients. Fresh shellfish, one of the most delicious of all tastes, needs little in the way of elaborate preparation or cooking.

One of my favourite cooking methods is grilling – the results are even more delicious when you cook and eat outside.

While the restaurant kitchen, with its gleaming stainless-steel surfaces and racks of equipment, has had an undoubted influence on contemporary kitchen design, good quality pots, pans, baking dishes and casseroles and a basic range of utensils are all that most people really need.

stainless-steel balloon whisk or pestle and mortar, and such necessities have changed very little for generations.

Whatever you collect beyond the range of such essential tools should reflect what you like to cook, which in turn should reflect what you like to eat. If you love oriental food, it makes sense to have a wok; a pasta-maker might come in handy if you are a devotee of Italian cooking. Apart from such exceptions, basic kitchen equipment is all most of us really need. It is not only tried and tested, but it offers precisely that down-to-earth quality that makes cooking so pleasurable and rewarding in the first place.

Coping with the bare minimum in holiday homes can provide a vivid illustration of this point. Suzie Slesin has been taking holidays on the same small Greek island for many years. Her tiny house, generally filled to bursting with family and friends, has the most rudimentary facilities: cooking (on two small hot plates) always takes place outside; ingredients come from the relatively narrow range of produce the island

Kitchen style should arise
naturally out of the integrity of
the materials used for surfaces
and finishes. This old-fashioned
French kitchen has a simple,
cheerful domesticity.

s to offer; equipment is improvised. Every year she sets herself the challenge of
ooking at least one meal that everyone can eat together – and what might seem
perficially a vexing and frustrating exercise always proves hugely enjoyable.

As the *batterie de cuisine* as status symbol reveals, kitchen style and aesthetics
n have more to do with impressing the neighbours than true ease of use or basic
nctionalism. In this idiom, you get kitchens designed to resemble high-tech
boratories, gleaming stainless-steel temples of hygiene and soulless efficiency,
, at the opposite end of the spectrum, kitchens decked out in all manner of pseudo-
lwardian accoutrements, with appliances concealed behind bespoke wooden
nels laden with twiddly decorative mouldings. Elizabeth David had her own
edictably tart views on the subject: 'I recoil from coloured tiles and beflowered
rfaces and I don't want a lot of things coloured avocado and tangerine. I'll just
ttle for the avocados and tangerines in a bowl on the dresser. In other words, if
e food and cooking pots don't provide enough visual interest and create their own
nanging patterns in a kitchen, then there's something wrong.'

If you keep practicality and the working nature of the kitchen in mind, style
ill look after itself. More than any other area in the home, kitchen surfaces and
nishes have jobs to do. They must be robust enough to stand wear, resistant to
xtremes of heat, steam and water, easy to clean and non-slip. In many people's
yes, this might constitute an argument in favour of synthetic materials, laminato
orktops, vinyl flooring and the like. I think, however, that artificial materials are, if
nything, more depressing in the kitchen than anywhere else, where they jar
ncomfortably with the vitality of taste, flavour and aroma that good cooking is all
bout. A certain hysterical paranoia about hygiene lies behind many decisions to
ubstitute synthetics for the real thing, but it is often an unwarranted and misinformed
nxiety. Linoleum, for example, a wholly natural product, actually scores higher as
n anti-bacterial material than vinyl, and looks, ages and performs infinitely better.
late shelves and stone floors provide a natural degree of refrigeration for larders
nd pantries; wooden worktops, butcher's blocks and chopping boards acquire a
elicious aroma after years of contact with the pungent flavours of garlic, onion
nd ginger, a smell that is as pleasing as their visual patina.

Time and distance are built into the whole experience of cooking today. Instead
f the daily stroll through the local market, there is the weekly shop at the superstore.
ood is chilled, frozen or held in stock until we can no longer really remember the
npulse of appetite that made us buy it in the first place. Cooking areas outside,
vhere you can recapture the unaffected simplicity of the outdoor trattoria or taverna,
nd vegetable patches, fruit trees and herb gardens, where you can harvest minutes
efore you eat, remind us how pleasurable it is when the journey from plough to
late is very much shorter. It is this immediacy that spells easy living to me.

**Eating in the kitchen, unthinkable in polite circles a half-century ago,
preserves the sense of immediacy that good, simple cooking is all about.**

eat

Eating outdoors is one of life's greatest pleasures – and you don't need a fully accessorized picnic hamper so stuffed with matching crockery that there is little room left for anything else – a simple basket will do. Failing that, an open doorway or even an open window, preferably looking out on to a garden, brings the same sense of vitality to indoor eating.

If you ever want to feel hungry, I suggest you read *The Wind in the Willows* by Kenneth Grahame. There is a great deal of eating in that book, much of it outdoors. The Rat's 'fat, wicker luncheon-basket' was not laden down with matching sets of crockery and cutlery but cold chicken,'coldtonguecoldham coldbeefpickledgherkinssaladfrenchrollscresssandwidges pottedmeatgingerbeerlemonadesodawater–', while the simple picnic he prepared for the adventuring Sea Rat, who sometimes woke up crying when he dreamed of 'the shell-fish of Marseilles', consisted of 'a yard of long French bread, a sausage out of which the garlic sang, some cheese which lay down and cried, and a long-necked straw-covered flask containing bottled sunshine . . . .' Perfect easy living.

Judging by the lovingly detailed descriptions of breakfasts, lunches and high teas that litter the book, from the first picnic on the river to the lobster salad supper at Toad Hall, Kenneth Grahame obviously enjoyed food very much. And as he was evidently aware, food tastes even better when you're sitting in a grassy spot with dappled light coming through the trees, or in a sheltered cove beside the sea with the waves gently crashing on the beach. One of the most memorable and most comfortable meals of my life took place one evening on a beach in the south of France. We sat eating round a big table, scrunching bare toes into the soft, warm sand while a huge crackling bonfire fuelled by broken beach chairs threw fantastic shapes into the night sky. Even the couscous tasted delicious.

Unfortunately, such experiences do not come along very often, but when they do, they illustrate the profound effect that our surroundings can have on our enjoyment of food.

As a restaurateur, I know how important the setting can be. It isn't merely a question of atmosphere. The dishes, jugs, glasses, plates and the knives and forks you use, the chairs you sit on and the table you sit at are the more functional sides of the matter. Eating itself is not really a function, of course, except in the prosaic sense of refuelling, but it does involve the consideration of certain practical factors that can significantly enhance, or undermine, what is one of the most basic of pleasures. Cooking takes care of what you eat; how and where are just as important.

I personally enjoy eating in a room that is open to other activities. In my house in the country, the kitchen is located in what was once a snooker room and there is plenty of space for a big table adjoining the area where the actual cooking takes place. It is certainly the most used room in the house.

In my apartment in London, cooking, eating and living areas flow into one another in an open-plan arrangement. Eating, I believe, is at its best when it is a communal experience and multi-function spaces help to promote a sense of generosity and hospitality. And when it isn't a communal experience, when you are eating alone, it is much more pleasant to do so in a space that is integrated with the rest of the home. A separate dining room, on the other hand, is a faintly ridiculous, if not miserable, place to munch your way through a solitary supper, which is why people who have separate dining rooms tend to have more easy-going eating areas in the kitchen as well.

I am far from unusual in my tastes; the dining room as a separate entity is on the wane, as it has been ever since entertaining gained a new informality in the 1960s. Nowadays, as a relic from more hierarchical times, a separate dining room can convey a rather ponderous sense of occasion, which is at odds with everyday mealtimes. Gone are the days (in most households, anyway) when the 'little woman' toiled behind a closed kitchen door while guests sipped indifferent sherry in the drawing room waiting for the summons to sit at the dining table – where they would find, no doubt, the seating plan enshrined on neat little place cards. Ever since the kitchen door first opened, wafting out tantalizing aromas and the excited hubbub of activity, it has never really closed again. The conviviality of supper round a table within reach of the stove and second helpings, and the refusal to stand on ceremony define social customs today.

I could choose to have a separate dining room if I wished – in fact, in the country I do have one, but it is rarely used. But for most people, such an arrangement is simply an inefficient and unaffordable use of space, since for much of the time the dining room stands empty. When such high demands are placed on every square inch of our homes, the separate dining room begs to be annexed for some harder-working purpose and it often isn't long before it is. What is equally unsatisfactory is the type of atmosphere that tends to be generated by leaving a room unoccupied for much of the day. Like all underused spaces, dining rooms can

The finesse of porcelain, smooth as an eggshell, adds a sense of refinement and delicacy to the table. I also enjoy the no-nonsense functionalism of Duralex tumblers, which are perfect for the job as well as being virtually unbreakable.

bbornly resist the attempt to bring them to life; something
a dead quality always seems to linger. Suzie Slesin, who
s to entertain quite large numbers of people at a moment's
ice, has a separate dining room to make this possible, but
e has kept the space alive by fitting it out as a library. Books
ate a companionable, clubby background for eating and
en the room is not serving its dedicated function, it can be
ed as a place for work and study.

An open-plan arrangement, however, does not mean
t activities literally have to run into each other. Eating
quires a different mood from cooking and there must be
ne separation between the two. You need to be able to pull
t your chair without crashing into a wall, or serve a meal
hout winding your way round obstacles. At the same time,
en you actually sit down to eat you need the intimacy of
table, the closed circle of companionship, with reminders
other functions fading into the background. Dining areas
ed some clear space, both physically and mentally.

L-shaped areas or those converted from two former
oms offer a natural division of space. Alternatively, you can
sition the table within the embrace of a bay window, or
the other side of a half-height counter that serves as a
rtial screen for kitchen activities.

Lighting plays a huge role in creating the right
nosphere. Dimmable background light, combined with small
wnlights focused on the table, provide a versatile
rangement for eating – provided you do not intend to alter
position of the table at some future date. A row of small
ndent lights can also be effective, but you must take care
ensure that the actual light sources are either shielded in
ne way or recessed deep enough within the fittings so as
t to cause glare. Lighting the table properly means using
surface as a gentle form of reflection, so that diners are
dazzled or oppressed by a relentless overhead glare. Light
unced off the table to light people from below is the most
ttering form of illumination.

Basic comfort and ease demands a sturdy table that is
enough for everyone to sit round, and chairs that are
ble, supportive and at the right height. Highly polished or

tableware, I am attracted to clean lines and simple forms. Teapots and jugs should pour
operly, cups feel right when you grip the handle and plates sit evenly on the table.

veneered finishes, such as the mahogany acreage of the traditional formal table, do not spell easy living to me: one watermark or fingerprint and the furniture wax has to come out again. Nor am I particularly fond of glass in this context (much as I love glass). Glass tables, when they are used for eating rather than display, can have a distinctly edgy quality which some people find as uncomfortable as the sound of fingernails drawn across a blackboard. Scrubbed oak, or some other good quality hardwood make infinitely more tolerant surfaces and do not require constant vigilance. Such tables are good-looking in their own right but robust enough to do duty as a place where homework can be tackled between mealtimes. In the same way, it is important to pay attention to the way dining chairs feel when you sit on them. Surprisingly, plenty of people don't. Chairs chosen on the basis of appearance alone can often make you want to leave the table faster than lumps in the sauce or a droning bore on your left. But comfort does not have to be taken to excess – people often forget that you lean forward when you eat, so you don't need a deeply padded back rest.

Tableware has long been the focus of much snobbery and status-seeking, with elaborate dinner services embellished with gilt and rampant patterns of fruit and vegetables featuring on many wedding lists. But plates that are fancier and more colourful than the food on them seem to miss the point. Real luxury for me comes from the quality of materials and the skill employed in their manufacture. White porcelain, for example, is absolutely right for the job and a pleasure to use. Smooth, so there are no grating sounds from knife or fork; thin, to provide a sense of finesse; and unadorned to keep the attention where it belongs – on the food – such tableware has an inherent feeling of quality, not a self-proclaimed price tag. I also enjoy the sort of robust crockery you find in restaurants and cafés, not the gritty rusticity of earthenware which is much too rough to eat off comfortably, but simple basic plates and dishes that are more likely to bounce than break if you drop them. Similarly, I like both plain, thin wine glasses, tapered and shaped to deliver the bouquet to your nose, and the down-to-earth quality of chunky Duralex tumblers – forms that are firmly based on

Some form of shade is vital for outdoor eating areas, especially in a hot climate. This canvas awning (far left) gives protection from the sun and has an appropriately nautical flavour for a balcony overlooking the sea.

The presentation of food should whet the appetite, not trumpet one's status. Simple containers, plain crockery, a white cloth and properly weighted cutlery allow the food you are serving to take centre stage.

function, just as the insulating thickness of a coffee cup is designed to maintain the heat of a drink we sip slowly, and the eggshell delicacy of a teacup helps to cool a drink we find more thirst-quenching.

I am not such a purist that I would forswear all touches of colour: a blue rim on a plate, for example, can sharpen and freshen the whole look, and patterns that add a feeling of vitality without dominating can also be very attractive. Strong solid colours can provide unbeatable accents on the table: a deep indigo bowl makes a pile of lemons or limes come alive; a tomato salad on a fresh green plate is incredibly appetizing. Such jolts of contrast heighten our awareness of food – think of Elizabeth David's Venetian market.

Utensils and cutlery when they are well designed provide a small satisfaction whenever we encounter them. Knives and forks should be weighted and balanced so they feel physically right in the hand, neither so light and flimsy you feel as if you can't put pressure on them, nor so heavy that you notice the effort of picking them up. It should be easy

Fresh food, simply served from the oven or grill to the table creates a welcome immediacy of experience.

Eating should be a convivial activity, where people relax and enjoy the company as much as what they eat. I much prefer plain white porcelain, generously proportioned, to patterned dinner services that are more colourful than the food.

to pour from a jug or teapot without splashing or dripping; the angle of a ladle should match the curving action of your wrist. These may seem like small points – details – but a sense of ease and enjoyment depends on them.

There is pleasure in basic contact with food, whether you are choosing it, preparing it or eating it. John Torode believes that 'if you plan too much, everything will end up too stilted', and that it is much better to go to the market with an open mind and allow yourself to become inspired by what is fresh and in season. I agree with him entirely and practise this principle wherever possible. From that selection process of touching and looking to cooking and eating, the important thing is to keep a relaxed attitude. When he has friends for supper, he puts big pots of food in the middle of the table and big spoons for people to help themselves. Crockery is deep white plates from a seconds' shop and Japanese noodle bowls; cutlery is plain bone-handled knives and forks bought in bundles from a market stall. 'I don't think we even have a tablecloth,' he says. 'It's a matter of sitting back and enjoying it. And the enjoyment comes from conversation and people as much as the food that brings them together.'

work

Basic household chores, from washing dishes to sweeping up, do not have to be drudgery. With the right tools, they can provide a type of relaxation: the chance to change gear and engage a different part of the mind.

Work, on the face of it, would seem to have little to do with easy living. If easy living, in its putting-your-feet-up sense, is everything we like doing, work must be everything else. But whether it takes the form of ironing the clothes, balancing the books or writing a report, work is an inevitable part of nearly everyone's life, and it only makes sense to arrange things so it can be as pleasant as possible.

I enjoy working, and I enjoy working at home. I particularly enjoy working in the garden on a sunny summer's day, sitting in a slightly battered wicker chair, with a good cigar, a glass of wine, a pad of paper and a 3B pencil close at hand. No noise, no interruptions, just the faint scent of roses: if this sounds like easy living, it is, but it is also the best way I know of getting the creative juices to flow. Pleasant surroundings free the mind. Why else do you have so many good ideas in the bath?

You can, in theory, work anywhere. In practice, it helps if there aren't children running in and out, doorbells ringing and messages stacked up on the answerphone.

'A room of one's own' was Virginia Woolf's prescription for a creative working life. Her advice was specifically intended for women; when she wrote the essay in which she aired these views, a woman may have been the mistress of her household but she often lacked any truly personal space within it.

Like many writers – Roald Dahl and Dylan Thomas included among them – Virginia Woolf was a devotee of the garden shed or hut as a thinking space. Most of us tend to work hardest when we are released from the complexities of routines, schedules and appointments; the studio, the workshop and the shed are all working rooms that provide this fundamental level of non-intervention. Unlike the factory floor, office or boardroom, they are not places to dread or shun; instead, they seem to have an irresistible lure. Tucked away at the bottom of the garden, far from the incessant ring of the telephone or the casual interruptions of daily life, the essence of the shed is the lack of distraction.

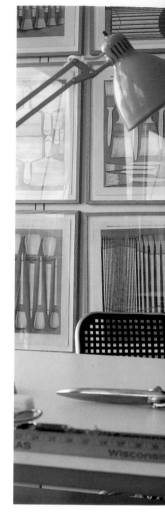

A dedicated work room is more or less essential if you are pursuing a career from home, but there is no need to import the office aesthetic. A wall of shelving provides systematic organization for books and files in a spacious work room (above). **In my study at home in London, rows of closely hung prints of brushes and tools put me in the mood for work** (above centre).

Lack of distraction owes as much to a certain simplicity of surroundings as it does to seclusion of location. Dahl's writing shed, where he worked sitting under heaps of blankets in cold weather with a drawing board on his lap and copious supplies of chocolate to hand, was more eccentric and perhaps more basic than most, but arranging things to suit yourself is the point at issue. Philippe Starck is one person I know who also finds he is at his most creative and productive when he deliberately puts himself in a position where he lives very simply. Focusing on the task at hand becomes easier when other layers of life are peeled away.

Escaping to the garden or shed is one way of working at home. For more organized home businesses, a slightly more professional version of the shed idea may be necessary to provide clients with a separate access that does not offer unwelcome glimpses of your domestic life. A dedicated work room or area can be particularly important if your livelihood depends upon it. In an office, it is easy enough to kid yourself that simply being there in some way constitutes working. With no one to call time on your coffee breaks, or monitor your personal phone calls, or point out that weeding the vegetable patch may be work but it isn't the same as completing the order by next Tuesday, lack of distraction can make all the difference between sinking and swimming. A work room or study won't make you self-disciplined all by itself, but it will close the door on peripheral temptations.

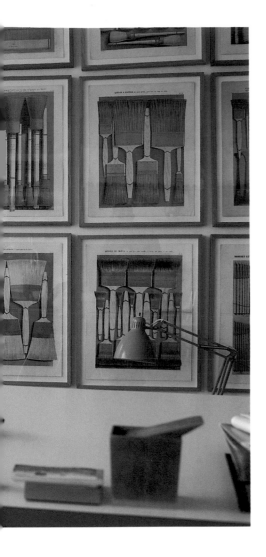

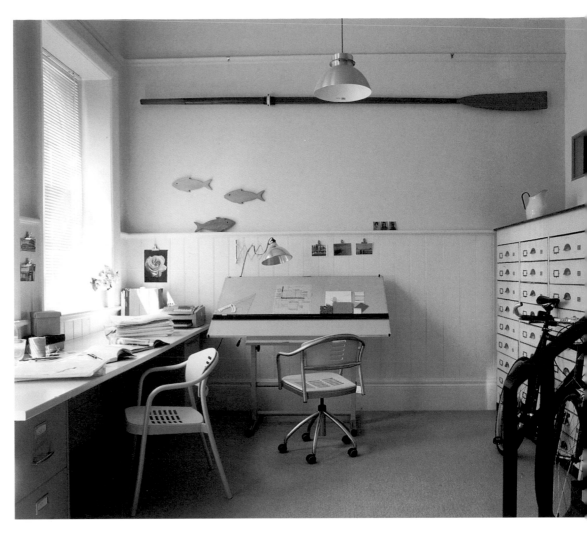

But with separate rooms in short supply in most households, some form of integration of home and working life is inevitable for many people. The question is how you achieve the same quality of concentration when you must work in areas that also serve other purposes. When work space shrinks to desk space, you need to be able to set up some form of psychological barrier between yourself and the rest of the home, which means choosing a location where interruptions are less likely and every square inch of space is not in competition from other activities: such as an alcove in a living area, a dining area between mealtimes or a workspace created from part of a bedroom. Where an area is devoted to different activities, a physical separation, such

as a screen, divider or a half-width partition, can make a lot of difference, creating a suggestion of enclosure which provides room for thought. But perhaps the most important element is a desk or bureau that can expand while you are working, then swallow up your work when you close it down.

The joy of working from home is that it offers the opportunity to create an environment that is personal, congenial and comfortable, instead of one that displays the same lowest-common-denominator functionalism you left behind with the numbered parking space and key to the executive washroom. As working from home becomes more of a social trend and less of a euphemism for skiving off, there is also an increasing need to reconcile the professional with

A study at home can be a spare room, an attic, a basement or a converted garage – ideally out of the main run of things. The point is to tailor the space to create the right working conditions for you. This studio (above)**, with tables arranged to benefit from the natural light, provides room for the personal touches discouraged in most offices.**

If you don't have enough room for a separate study or home office, space will need to be found in an area where other activities take place. In such instances, the right conditions are even more important to gain the necessary psychological separation from the rest of the household.

A desk placed at a window, so that you sit with your back to the rest of the room, is one arrangement that can help concentration. A comfortable chair to support your back and at the right height for the work surface is essential.

the domestic: spreading your papers over the kitchen table or parking your pens in an empty tin with the label soaked off might do for a while, but eventually you need to show you mean business – if only yourself. How you arrange and equip your workspace and the accessories you choose to accompany can help to bridge the gap between the home-in-the-office and the office-in-the-home.

Work that is primarily desk-bound may not require much in the way of surrounding space beyor what is required to house files, books, papers and other supplies. But the quality of the immediate workin area is critical. Decent light, both natural and artificial, a comfortable chair, a sound work surface and a infrastructure of power and phone lines are essential.

Many people equip a study or work area with cast-off office equipment or designs that share th same defiantly harsh aesthetic, an approach that may indicate they are missing the office more than the care to admit. This seems a huge pity to me, when there are so many alternatives that function just a effectively, if not more so, but offer a much higher degree of pleasure in use. A sturdy wooden table of th right height is infinitely more enjoyable to work at than a flimsy prefabricated workstation and it supplie a material dimension that helps to humanize work. At the same time, many pieces of functional equipme have an inherent rightness of design, which can be equally appealing. A well-made steel filing cabine which can be pushed under the table, or an Anglepoise lamp are hard-working designs with a pleasin simplicity of use and appearances that fit easily into a domestic environment.

Free-standing screens can be an invaluable way of segregating space and providing some privacy for work requiring peace and quiet. A screen composed of translucent panels allows light to filter through (left).

The right type of lighting is particularly important for computer work. Natural light coming from behind the screen prevents glare while a task light can be angled to direct light at the keyboard.

When working from home, you can usually choose the level of technology that is most appropriate and productive for you. I prefer a pen with a free flow of ink or a good sharp pencil when it comes to sketching out ideas.

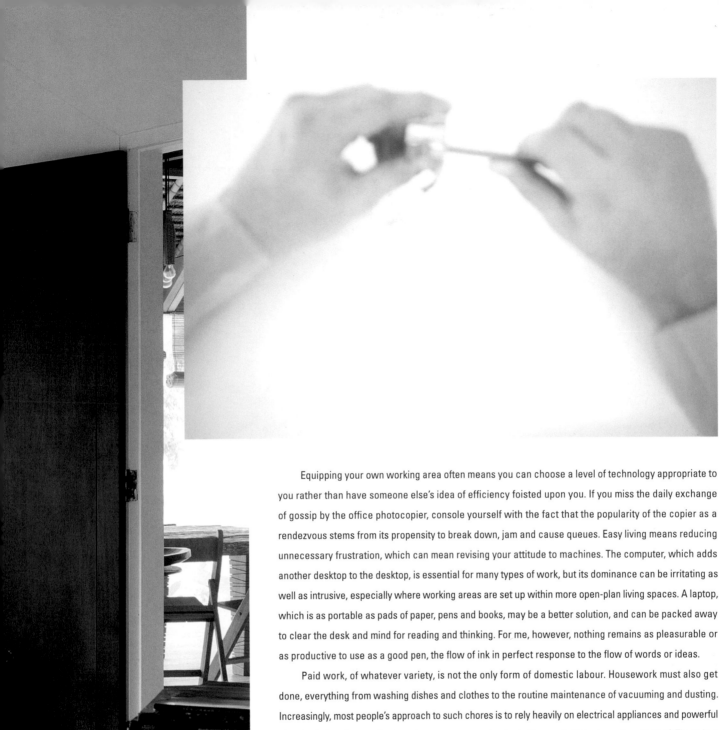

Equipping your own working area often means you can choose a level of technology appropriate to you rather than have someone else's idea of efficiency foisted upon you. If you miss the daily exchange of gossip by the office photocopier, console yourself with the fact that the popularity of the copier as a rendezvous stems from its propensity to break down, jam and cause queues. Easy living means reducing unnecessary frustration, which can mean revising your attitude to machines. The computer, which adds another desktop to the desktop, is essential for many types of work, but its dominance can be irritating as well as intrusive, especially where working areas are set up within more open-plan living spaces. A laptop, which is as portable as pads of paper, pens and books, may be a better solution, and can be packed away to clear the desk and mind for reading and thinking. For me, however, nothing remains as pleasurable or as productive to use as a good pen, the flow of ink in perfect response to the flow of words or ideas.

Paid work, of whatever variety, is not the only form of domestic labour. Housework must also get done, everything from washing dishes and clothes to the routine maintenance of vacuuming and dusting. Increasingly, most people's approach to such chores is to rely heavily on electrical appliances and powerful chemical cleaning products, or to pay someone else to do the work. But where does it stop? There is a new trend for 'cash-rich, time-poor' Californians to employ other people to manage virtually every aspect of their lives, from scheduling dental appointments to choosing a new house and moving all their belongings into it. The understandable aim is to save time and effort, but the result can be a frantic acceleration of life as you try to pack more and more into the day, while a mania for delegation risks turning you into little more than a house guest In your own home. Curiously, many overstressed high-fliers who go off to remote hillside farmhouses on spiritual 'retreats' frequently find that activities they would normally perceive as

drudgery, such as washing up and sweeping floors, can suddenly take on an almost Zen-like significance. When the surroundings are basic and there isn't a vacuum cleaner for miles, enlightenment can take the surprising form of rediscovering the soothing quality of simple work.

Few of us are prepared to forgo modern convenience entirely, but an improved quality of living can be achieved by ensuring that the places where work must be done and the tools which we use are as decent and well designed as possible. If the kitchen has shed its dreary, neglected aesthetic in recent years, many utility areas are still in the Dark Ages. There is no reason why this should be so. A dark laundry room is a miserable place to wash clothes and linen; a crumbling cobwebbed shed full of tangled garden implements won't inspire you when it comes to spring planting. Taking care over such behind-the-scenes spaces goes a long way to putting you in the right mood for work.

Plain functional tools for indoors and out, from laundry baskets and dustpans to rakes and spades, also minimize frustration and introduce the ease that comes from pleasure of use. They feel right in the hand, they perform well and they last

The artist's studio – with props and incidental objects to spark the imagination, brushes, paints and tools to hand and room to make a mess – is the ultimate creative working space. Drenched in natural light, this glowing room is the studio of the British artist Patrick Heron (left).

The shed is every gardener's favourite haunt. But a surprising number of artists and writers have also found the shed to be a convenient creative retreat. George Bernard Shaw's writing hut in his garden at Ayot St Lawrence sat on a rotating pedestal so that the entire shed could be swivelled round to face the sun.

contrast, the ironing board that collapses in a shrieking metallic wheeze every e you try to put it up, or the vacuum cleaner that coughs up piles of dust, or the ush that stubbornly refuses to remain attached to its handle erode any small isfaction one might derive from basic daily chores. The Shakers, whose dedication work was an integral part of their religious philosophy, understood the value of od tools; their tools and fittings, from brooms to pegboards, display the same ality of loving craftsmanship that is prized in their furniture. It also helps if what u are maintaining – whether it's a tabletop or floor – is made of the type of material

that does not require constant niggling vigilance and titivating to remain vaguely attractive. Real materials that age well often also clean and keep well.

Many types of work have the potential to provide a great deal of satisfaction: easy living, at times, may be less about avoiding work altogether and more about enjoying whatever you do. It is interesting that many of us choose to relax, not by lying comatose under a pile of Sunday papers, but by actively engaging in some other form of activity. Gardening, cooking, even cleaning can provide an invigorating change of gear, the chance to engage another part of the mind.

detail

my introduction, I referred to Vita Sackville-West's list of personal pleasures, her catalogue of 'through leaves'. Detail in the home works in a similar fashion. It offers the same sort of smooth, seamless operation of a well-made drawer or well-oiled lock but it also provides flashes of pure pleasure that are no less agreeable for being unmomentous. A fleeting view from a landing window, scented flowers, light shining through coloured glass and dappling the floor – such details create a sense of place as much as the larger matters of decor and design. Their essence is surprise, and a certain transience. The view you catch out of the corner of your eye as you pass by remains intriguing far longer than the static panorama of a picture window. Fresh flowers provide more delight in the week or two of their short lives than the dried arrangements that sit ignored and dusty all year round. Detail, as the expression of personality and taste, is the heart and soul of easy living.

Details, however, can trip you up. If God is in them, so, too, is the devil. Before architects sign off new buildings, they have to undertake an often tedious fault-finding mission in which they tour the site, noting every deficiency – cracks, substandard workmanship, missing handles, unpainted guttering – so that the shortfalls can be made good before the final handover. The term for this process is 'snagging' and it describes perfectly the kind of minor aggravation that catches your attention just long enough to annoy you but, all too often, not really long enough for you to fix it. A dripping tap, a drawer that won't close properly, a loose floorboard, an overstuffed cupboard whose contents spill out every time you open the door are all 'details' that can stand in the way of easy living.

Inertia may be one reason why we put up with such vexations and put off the day when we intend to tackle them; another might be an acknowledgment of the innate awkwardness of inanimate objects, or, as in that French phrase quoted by Vita Sackville-West, *la méchanceté des choses* – the naughtiness of things. The inherent waywardness of the string that always gets tangled in the bottom of the drawer or the lid of the butter dish that always gets mislaid is closely related to the law of household perversity that states that if you take the trouble to fix one thing, two things will break the next day. Minor failures of function, however, are an inevitable side effect of use and wear; handles work loose, doors swell, paint peels off and cupboards become silted with clutter. Unlike an architect who can turn a job over to a client and hopefully be done with it, it's better to accept that in most homes 'snagging' is an on-going process. Making the effort to put small things right from time to time pays enormous dividends in making living easier.

It goes without saying that what is gimcrack, rickety and flimsy in the first place won't stand much chance of surviving even a regular dose of wear and tear. Most people are inclined to learn the hard way and this persuasive argument in favour of investing in quality at the outset, or at least in the best you can afford, seems to hit home only after you've gone the long way round.

Detail, as the hallmark of good design, is revealed in the quality of workmanship and functional performance, the degree of extra care that shows itself slowly over time. Strong, well-made hinges capable of bearing the weight of a door without buckling, the reassuring grip of handles that truly fit the hand, locked seams that delay fraying, the angle of a spout that pours right every time are not accidental presences, but the result of a thoughtful design process. Attention to this kind of detail is hugely important to me. Whether we're designing something new for the shops or buying

in products from elsewhere, every item is subject to the same intense scrutiny and analysis. Does it work properly? How does it feel when you hold it? Will it tip over too easily if you brush against it? Does it mark or stain too readily? Will it age gracefully? As a consumer, it is equally important to weigh alternatives and second-guess how something will work and look, not just the first time you use it, but the fifty-first time as well.

In a wider context, detail is both what you see and what you don't see. You shouldn't see pipes interrupting walls or snaking along at floor level, collecting dust and grease; neither should there be wires trailing across your path threatening to trip you up or lying in a tangled heap by an overloaded socket. It takes planning and effort to eliminate this type of unwelcome detail, but it is an essential part of getting the infrastructure of your home in order.

The interior detail with which most people are familiar is architectural or 'period': cornices, mouldings, ceiling roses, skirting boards, dado rails and architraves – the whole kit of historical parts. Interestingly, however, many such details, no matter how decorative they appear, were often originally conceived with rather more practical purposes in mind.

Architectural detail, in most people's minds, is synonymous with historic or period features. But it can also mean the extra degree of care taken over such seemingly minor points as edges, fittings and fixtures, switches, catches and handles. The sculptural sweep of a stair, lined in wood, relies on a precision finish; the smooth curve of a banister gives pleasure every time you use the stairs; the hearth remains a powerful focus in a contemporary space.

Everyone has their passions; one of mine is glass. Some of my collection is displayed on a table at the bottom of the stairs in my London apartment (left), top-lit by natural light spilling down from above. The fragility and translucence of certain flowers are another favourite and share similar qualities – characteristics enhanced by light.

The skirting board, for example, may appear, on a superficial level, to be a comfortable finishing touch, lending definition to the junction between the two planes of the wall and the floor. More prosaically, it exists as an acknowledgment of how extremely difficult it is to achieve a straight edge in plaster or to allow the exact margin for shrinkage or building movement; it's a cover-up, in other words. Minimalists, who prefer their walls to remain unadorned, with razor-sharp edges, will tell you how expensive and laborious it can be to do without this kind of detail. In the same way, cornicing, whether it is Georgian egg-and-dart or Victorian wedding cake, disguises the inevitable cracking that occurs where plastered wall meets plastered ceiling.

Perhaps the most cherished architectural detail of all is the fireplace. In the past, of course, it was hardly a detail, more the central practicality of the home, where food was cooked, washing water boiled and enough warmth generated to make the grind of daily life tolerable. As a gathering place or focus (the literal meaning of 'hearth'), the fireplace has long had a powerful hold on our emotions. We don't need a fireplace when we have central heating – in fact, one would have to turn the heating down to enjoy a real fire without sweltering – but huddling up to a radiator on a cold day just doesn't have the same appeal. The sight of flames flickering in the hearth or behind the glass door of a wood-burning stove adds a sense of vitality as well as a soothing reassurance; the smell of woodsmoke is one of the most evocative aromas I know, and the television is certainly no substitute.

Anything you hang on the wall,
whether family photographs,
a child's scribbles or leaves
collected on a walk, assumes
importance. A massed display
has graphic impact, but casual
propping on a tabletop, shelf or
chest can be just as effective.
Pictures hung in corners, on side
or flanking walls, or where the
eye glimpses them in passing,
surprise and delight for longer
than those on prominent display.

As people have rather belatedly come to realize, stripping away such original features is both counter-productive and unsightly. Old rooms with traces of their past surgically removed often look unbalanced and disjointed; what's missing is not merely a decorative flourish but a way of making sense of scale and proportion. The reverse – slotting off-the-peg features into a plain modern room – results in a different sense of unease. Stick-on cornices and chair rails tacked at some arbitrary point halfway up the wall may promise instant history, but no one is really fooled – architectural detail should be a natural expression of the basic character of your home.

There is another type of architectural detail that has to do with finesse. The banister that is uninterrupted by clumsy supports, so your hand can slide smoothly all the way from top to bottom, is as lovely to touch as it is to look at. The neat finish where two different types of flooring meet is both practical – preventing materials from lifting or chipping – and visually pleasing. The extra attention paid to minor points, such as socket and switch covers, door knobs and catches, invests everything with a feeling of thoughtfulness and care.

At the same time, detail is all about pleasure. On the level of enjoyment, it embraces wit, surprise and personal expression: the imagination in free play. Things that exist purely for their own sake – a bowl of lemons, a bunch of fragrant flowers, photographs of family and friends, and paintings – add pure joy in small doses and life would be much poorer without them.

Some of the most evocative objects are handmade. Handblown glass, for example, possesses none of the mechanical uniformity of a factory product, but retains a hint of the organic fluidity of molten glass itself. Similarly, handthrown pots express the plasticity of raw clay, the sense in which the material shapes what you can do with it. In the slight irregularity of appearance and feel, such objects connect us directly with the process of making. You can almost see the intuitive choreography of the glassblower or feel the centrifugal force of the wheel pulling on the potter's hands. When so much else in the world comes off a production line, we need such reminders of human creativity around us.

Working detail makes the difference between life running smoothly and constant frustration. It may lie in the thoughtfulness of design, such as the lipped rim of a tray that allows it to be carried more easily, the exact fitting of wooden joints or the smooth operation of well-made drawers.

Whatever you display should express a similar sense of connection. Suzie Slesin, who is incredibly well travelled, has learned to recognize those elements that are 'strong in style, that have a point of view', objects that are embedded with a sense of place and authenticity. It is not a quality that can be simulated or imposed; it's personal and comes naturally when you have the courage of your convictions, when you select what you really like and 'go to the end of your feelings'.

Works of art – from a child's drawing to a sculpture or painting – have the same ability to convey meaning and feeling. So many displays are merely dreary expressions of what people think ought to be on view: hence, the timid rows of neatly framed, mass-produced botanical prints that might as well be hanging in the corridor of a provincial hotel for all the visual pleasure they generate. If buying a work of art sounds intimidating, a pursuit only for the rich or knowledgeable museum curators, bear in mind that many original pieces are not only well within the average person's financial reach but are readily accessible in local galleries, art schools and exhibitions. Investment potential has nothing to do with it at all. There will always be gas and electricity bills to pay, mortgage interest rate rises and other

Detail operates on both aesthetic
and practical levels. It is flowers
and decorative displays that
refresh and lift the spirits, but at
the same time it is also taps that
don't leak and floorboards and
hinges that don't squeak.

reasons why such purchases are not strictly prudent and sensible. It takes a certain leap of faith to buy or display what really moves you, but the result will give you pleasure on a daily basis and imbue your home with your personality.

Detail can be as ephemeral as a bowl of roses, a postcard propped on the mantelpiece, a snapshot of a favourite place, something that jogs your memory. Transience is the essence of such arrangements; they come and go. Flowers are Joseph's favourite things of all; against the neutral background of his home, they provide the living accent of colour. The joy, of course, is that such accents are always changing and it is the element of surprise that keeps interiors alive.

Massed in a simple container, on the desk, on the dining table, by the bedside, flowers lift the spirits like nothing else. I can think of nothing more likely to generate a mood of optimism than a vase full of white roses: beautiful form, generous simplicity and a gentle, instantly recognizable perfume.

The most important details of all are those that make your home yours and not anyone else's. They are the things that remind you of where you've been, what you've done, whom you've known and loved. They are the things that, if your house was on fire, your insurance was paid up and your family was safe, you would rescue. The close focus of detail identifies what makes life truly worth living.

The least inspiring displays are composed of objects you expect to see, or those that remain in the same dusty corner year after year. By contrast, objects that mean something to you, that enshrine memories of a favourite place or time or person, always have vitality: they actually have something to say. You can group objects by type, colour or texture, but there really are no hard-and-fast rules for display except to surround yourself with things you positively enjoy.

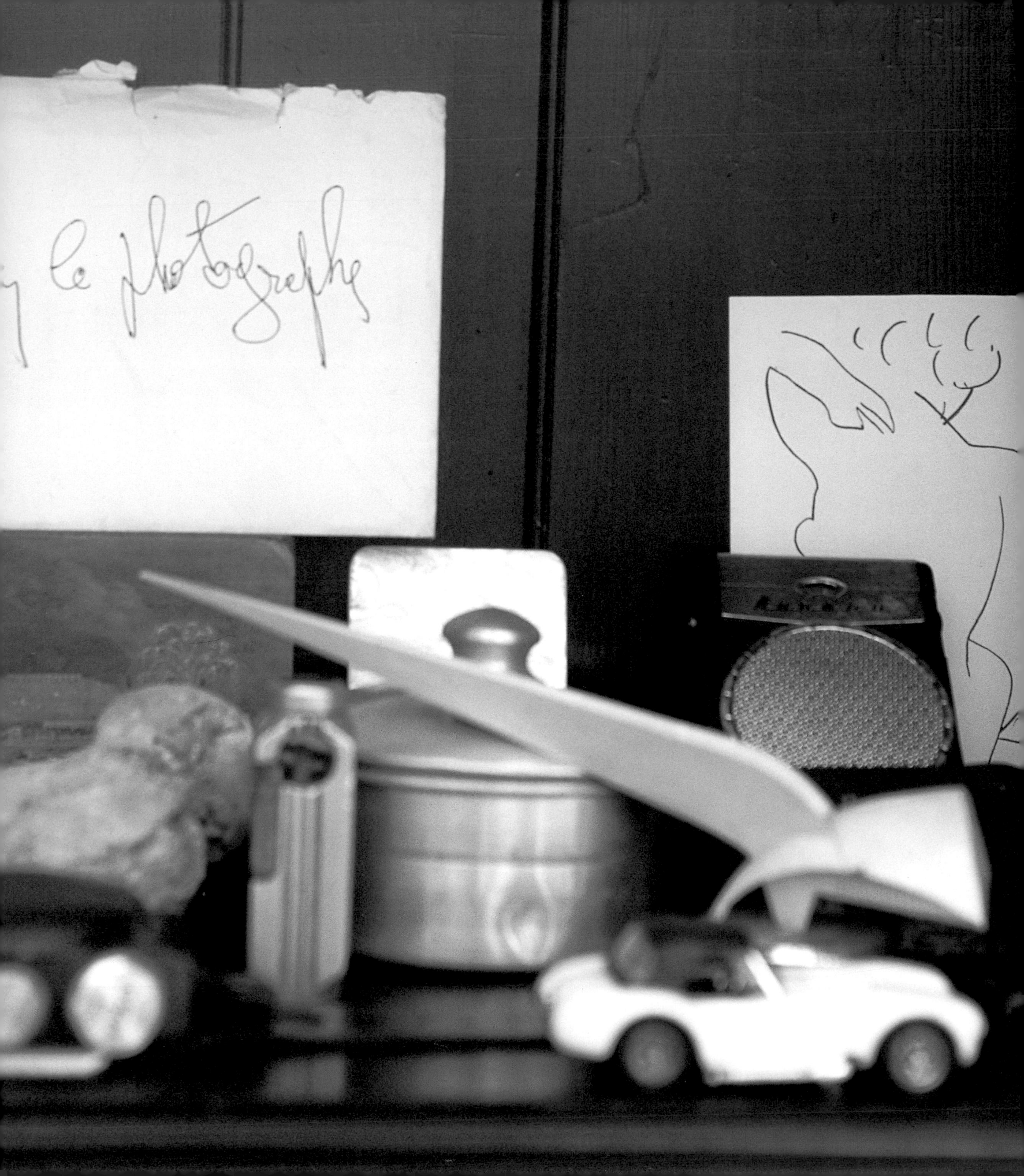
le photographe

index